Sanctity and Shadows The Unholy See

Allen Schery

BROOKLYN BRIDGE BOOKS

Brooklyn Bridge Books

DEDICATION

This book is dedicated to my mentors in History. Due to their Influence this is my third book regarding History. (The other two were about the Illuminati and the Knights Templar). My major focus has always been what I call Philosophical Anthropology as I am trained in Anthropology and Archeology. My mentors in History were Alice D'Addario and Romaine Francois Poirot at Walt Whitman High School and Benjamin Ruekberg and Regis Courtemanche at Post College. All are passed an do not know of their influence. I salute their essence through the ether of time.

Contents

Preface

Preface

The Genesis and Evolution of Papal Authority

In the vibrant mosaic of early Christianity, the evolution of centralized ecclesiastical authority unfolds as a sweeping epic—a gradual metamorphosis from a richly decentralized fellowship into a singular, revered institution that would shape the future of Western Christendom. In these formative years, the Church thrived on a collegial model where diverse communities flourished under local bishops' gentle yet spirited guidance. These bishops, esteemed custodians of apostolic tradition, nurtured congregations that were as regionally distinct as they were united by a common spiritual heritage. At the very heart of this unfolding drama stood Saint Peter, a luminous figure whose legacy radiated far beyond his earthly life. Revered not only as the rock upon which the Church was built but also as a martyr whose unwavering devotion illuminated the dark corridors of persecution, Peter's life and death laid an indelible foundation of faith—a foundation that would inspire and guide generations of believers. Nevertheless, the human hands that would build upon this sacred rock were themselves prone to frailty, ambition, and the corrupting influences of power, planting the first seeds of future conflict within the nascent institution.

Following Peter's illustrious footsteps, early shepherds like Linus and Clement I emerged as vital figures who bridged the era of the Apostles and the expansive, burgeoning faith community. Linus, venerated as one of Peter's earliest successors, provided a tangible link to the apostolic past, ensuring an unbroken chain of spiritual authority even as the Church navigated the turbulent waters of its infancy. His brief but pivotal tenure reassured believers during a time when uncertainty reigned supreme. Equally compelling was Clement I, whose pastoral leadership and erudite epistles—most notably his stirring letter to the Corinthians—left an enduring imprint on early Christian thought. Clement's writings eloquently balanced compassionate pastoral care with incisive doctrinal clarity, and the tradition of his martyrdom, replete with vivid narratives of sacrifice, further underscored his steadfast commitment to "the faith." These early leaders, steeped in the zeal of apostolic witness, set the stage for the eventual emergence of a more centralized and authoritative structure that, while intended for unity, would also become a crucible for human ambition.

However, even as these foundational figures nurtured "the faith" locally, the early Church was not immune to the pressures of an ever-changing geopolitical landscape. The sprawling Roman Empire, with its shifting alliances and power dynamics, provided both a challenging backdrop and a fertile ground for transformation. It was in this context that the dramatic conversion of Emperor Constantine emerged as a pivotal turning point—a moment that would forever alter the destiny of Christianity. In a legendary encounter prior to the decisive battle at the Milvian Bridge, Constantine is said to have witnessed a celestial vision accompanied by the resounding proclamation, "In hoc signo vinces" ("In this sign, you will conquer"). Whether interpreted as an unequivocal act of divine intervention or a sagacious political omen, its profound revelation transformed Constantine's heart. His conversion heralded the dawn of a new era in which the Christian faith was endowed with imperial legitimacy, thereby transforming it from a beleaguered sect into a preeminent force within the Roman state. However, this unprecedented convergence of spiritual mission with temporal power brought with it both immense opportunity and the seeds of profound moral compromise.

The transformative power of Constantine's conversion was far-reaching. No longer were Christian communities forced to exist in the shadows of persecution; instead, they began to receive the full backing of an empire that was both influential and far-sighted.

Constantine enacted sweeping reforms, such as the historic Edict of Milan, which granted religious tolerance across the empire and effectively liberated Christianity from the bonds of systemic oppression. This newfound patronage by the imperial power provided material and political support and paved the way for the establishment of theological clarity and unity. In the charged atmosphere of debates over doctrine and heresy, imperial support accelerated the convening of large-scale councils, most notably the Council of Nicaea in 325 AD. These gatherings were not merely administrative formalities; they became the crucible in which the essential tenets of faith were refined, debated, and ultimately codified. Through these deliberations, the seeds of a centralized ecclesiastical structure took root, gradually steering the Church toward an unequivocal commitment to orthodoxy. Nevertheless, the very mechanisms designed for control and uniformity would, at times, foster repression, ambition, and deviations from the spiritual path.

As the influence of Constantine's reforms rippled through the Christian world, the decentralized network of local congregations began to coalesce into a more unified institutional framework. The bishop of Rome, once primarily a custodian of local apostolic tradition, was gradually elevated into a role that would eventually be known as the Papacy. With the weight of imperial endorsement, the Roman episcopate transitioned from a symbolic vessel of apostolic continuity into a potent unifying force—aptly designated the "Vicar of Christ." This evolution was neither abrupt nor unchallenged; it was the product of prolonged theological debates, fervent liturgical practices, and the pragmatic demands of governing an ever-expanding faith community. The careful curation of orthodox teachings and the deliberate sidelining of apocryphal texts that threatened doctrinal consistency exemplified the clinical precision with which early church leaders responded to internal diversities. In doing so, they laid the groundwork for a centralized ecclesiastical authority that held sway over a mosaic of hitherto independent Christian communities. However, the capacity for its greatest abuses would paradoxically emerge within the immense power of this evolving office.

The period following Constantine's conversion witnessed an extraordinary confluence of spiritual fervor and political acumen. Bishops from prominent centers of early Christianity—such as Alexandria, Antioch, and Jerusalem—engaged in dynamic councils and liturgical reformations that underscored a vibrant, though still decentralized, interchange of ideas. While celebrating their unique theological and cultural identities, these regional assemblies increasingly recognized the pragmatic necessity of unity. The backdrop of imperial power and the ever-growing demands of doctrinal precision nurtured an environment in which the centralized authority of the Roman see could gradually assert itself. As controversies over Christ's nature, the relationship between divinity and humanity, and the interpretation of sacred texts intensified, the intellectual and spiritual leadership emanating from Rome proved to be both a beacon and a bulwark against the forces of fragmentation.

The brilliance of early Christian thought is perhaps most vividly illustrated in the writings and martyrdoms that flowed from this period—marked by both adversity and apostolic triumph. Saint Peter's legacy, immortalized not only through sacred scripture but also through the passionate retellings of later tradition, provided a template for what it meant to be an unwavering servant of truth. Linus and Clement I, with their humble yet resolute ministries, exemplified the enduring connection between the tangible past and an uncertain future. Their contributions were not isolated anecdotes; they were the luminous threads that, when woven together, created a tapestry of spiritual resilience and visionary leadership. This tapestry would, over time, become the very fabric upon which the papal institution was embroidered—a fabric that combined the warmth of local tradition with the rigor of universal doctrine.

As centuries passed, the dynamic interplay between decentralized community practices and the emerging centralization of ecclesiastical power continued to evolve. The gradual refinement of church governance, catalyzed by imperial patronage and the exigencies of doctrinal uniformity, spoke of a long and arduous journey that was as much about reconciling diversity as it was about forging a common identity. This evolution was underscored by the tireless efforts of countless early church leaders who recognized that the survival of "the faith" depended on a delicate balance between tradition and innovation. Their endeavors in meticulously curating a unified canon of scripture, educating the faithful through eloquent sermons and epistles, and facing the existential threats of doctrinal deviation, were instrumental in transforming a fragile movement into an enduring institution.

Constantine's conversion, in particular, stands out as one of the most dramatic turning points in this narrative—a moment when divine inspiration converged with human ambition to create a a new leadership paradigm. With the emperor's decisive embrace of Christianity, the religion was imbued with the authority of an entire empire. This unparalleled synthesis of spiritual and temporal power not only secured the Church's position within the political hierarchy but also ensured that its doctrines would be disseminated and defended with unprecedented vigor. The convocation of the Council of Nicaea, which brought together some of the most erudite minds of the time, is a testament to the new era of enlightened discourse that Constantine's patronage inaugurated. Here, amid fervent debates and impassioned appeals to orthodoxy, early Church leaders laid down the doctrinal markers that would define the trajectory of Christian thought for generations to come.

In retrospect, the transformation from a decentralized, locally grounded Church into the centralized Papacy is a narrative rich with nuance and historical significance. It is a story that encapsulates the resilience of early believers, the visionary leadership of ecclesiastical pioneers, and the transformative impact of imperial power—themes that continue to resonate in contemporary discussions of faith and governance. The journey was anything but linear: it was a labyrinthine process marked by moments of luminous clarity interspersed with periods of intense struggle and debate. The synthesis of local apostolic tradition with the sweeping reforms of imperial patronage ultimately forged an institution capable of transcending time and geography—a testament to the enduring human quest for spiritual unity amid diversity. However, a truly complete understanding of this monumental evolution demands that we also confront the challenging reality that not all who occupied the Chair of Peter lived up to its sacred ideals. It is within the human dimension of this divine office that we find the compelling stories of its 'holy woes'.

Today, as we reflect on this profound evolution, we witness the legacy of Saint Peter, Linus, and Clement I not only in the hallowed halls of the Vatican but also in the collective memory of a faith that endures. Their lives, replete with acts of martyrdom, heartfelt pastoral care, and fearless intellectual engagement, continue to inspire modern interpretations of leadership and authority. The story of how a persecuted minority transformed into a formidable institution through centralized governance and doctrinal unity offers timeless lessons about the nature of power, community resilience, and the transformative potential of spiritual insight. Yet, it also illuminates the profound moral dilemmas, political entanglements, and personal failings that have, at various junctures, cast shadows upon the sacred office.

Ultimately, the genesis and evolution of papal authority is a narrative that beckons further exploration. How did the theological debates of the early councils refine or redefine the contours of orthodoxy? In what ways did the interplay between regional diversity and centralized power influence subsequent European religious and political transformations? The journey from the humble beginnings of local apostolic leadership to the towering edifice of the Papacy is a rich tapestry—one that invites us to explore, question, and appreciate the intricate processes through which human institutions are born, evolve, and endure. This book embarks on such an exploration, specifically by examining those periods and pontificates where the human flaws of the office holders brought "holy woes" to the sacred office, offering a crucial dimension to the Papacy's complex and enduring story.

The papacy has always stood as a towering beacon of spiritual authority and moral guidance—a summit meant to exemplify integrity, sanctity, and divine purpose. However, this revered office has also borne witness to moments of profound human frailty and daunting controversy over the centuries. In each era, the papacy has had to navigate treacherous political waters, reconcile competing demands from secular and ecclesial spheres, and often bear the heavy burden of its imperfections.

In this book, we embark on a journey traversing history's labyrinth. Here, we explore the celebrated triumphs of papal leadership and the darker, controversial episodes that lie beneath the surface. From Pope Stephen VI's shocking cadaver trial to the perilous diplomacy enacted against totalitarian regimes in the 20th century, our voyage is one of rigorous inquiry into how faith and politics have long danced a controversial duet.

Drawing on primary documents, scholarly research, and timeless narratives, our work offers an honest exploration of power, legacy, and the human condition. We invite the reader to look beyond simplistic denunciations and instead appreciate the intricate tapestry wrought by ambition, belief, and historical circumstance. The interplay of light and shadow in these pages is, ultimately, the story of us all.

Chapter One
The Myth of Pope Joan

In the murky twilight of medieval Europe—a realm where whispered secrets and half-forgotten legends intertwined with the scant light of documented fact—the tale of Pope Joan emerged like a fabled apparition. It is a story steeped in mystery and defiance, a narrative that captures the imagination by recounting the purported rise of a woman who transcended the shackles of her gender. Disguised as a man, Joan stealthily ascended the ecclesiastical ladder to a position that, by all conventional measures, belonged exclusively to men. For a brief, astonishing interlude in the ninth century, she was said to have worn the papal mantle under the name John, challenging the strictures of her era and the very foundation of the Church's authority.

Set against a backdrop of political instability, shifting alliances, and feverish rumors, the environment of the early medieval world was as unstable as it was enchanting. The ninth century, now regarded as both formative and obscured by successive layers of myth, was when the boundary between truth and fable was as porous as the walls of a crumbling abbey. In an age when literacy was the privilege of only a few and oral traditions reigned supreme, stories of shocking papal intrigue spread like wildfire—exciting the minds of ordinary folk and dissenting scholars alike. Nevertheless, the testimony for a female pontiff is sparse; her legend survives in chronicles penned centuries after the time she was purported to have reigned, forcing modern historians to sift through relics of conjecture and fantastical lore.

The earliest surviving murmurs of Pope Joan's tale emerge from the thirteenth century. Chroniclers like Jean de Mailly first hinted at the existence of an enigmatic female pope, omitting even her name, while later writers such as Martin of Opava expanded the short account into a full-blown narrative. According to these sources, Joan was a woman of extraordinary intellect and determination—denied a formal education solely because of her gender, she assumed a male identity to gain entry into the realm of scholarly endeavor and clerical ambition. Over time, her story swelled from a mere curious mention to an epic saga. Legends claim that she advanced through the ranks of the Church, became a cardinal, and was ultimately elected pope—taking the name John (or, in some retellings, John VIII). These accounts herald her as an emblem of the extraordinary potential of a woman forced to maneuver through a rigid patriarchal order while also igniting debates about clerical celibacy, authority, and the moral underpinnings of the Church.

The narrative reaches a fever pitch in its most familiar rendition. At the height of an ecclesiastical crisis, when the Church itself trembled under the weight of internal strife, Joan—cloaked utterly in the guise of a man—was chosen to lead. For a seemingly miraculous span of two years, seven months, and four days from 853 to 855, she is said to have governed the realms of the faithful with an uncommon combination of wisdom and determination. An almost preternatural acumen marked her leadership as she guided the institution through precarious times. However, the brilliance of her secret could not remain concealed indefinitely. In a dramatic, almost cinematic moment during a public procession, the carefully constructed façade of male authority shattered when Joan gave birth—a revelation so jarring that it sparked immediate horror among the assembled clergy and laity alike. The shock of witnesses culminated in a swift and brutal reprisal: legends recount that she was lynched, her name expunged from official records in an instant of collective outrage.

Even as the vivid accounts of Pope Joan captivate the imagination, modern scholars eye her legend with a measured skepticism. Today, most historians consider the tale a composite myth—a narrative woven from the threads of political satire, cultural critique, and the innate human desire to challenge authority. The story's glaring anachronisms are many: there is a conspicuous void of reliable, contemporary evidence from when she was purported to have reigned, and the chronology laid out by later chroniclers stands at odds with the well-documented succession of popes. Many of the more sensational details first appear in texts written hundreds of years later, suggesting that the tale may have been concocted as a polemical weapon or a cautionary fable against ecclesiastical corruption.

By examining the ebb and flow of myth versus fact, historians have come to see the Pope Joan legend as an evolving tapestry of reinterpretation. In times of moral crisis and institutional decay, some within the Church might have embraced the idea of a female pope as a powerful metaphor—a stark, subversive image meant to highlight their leaders' hypocrisy and ethical shortcomings. In this light, the legend of Pope Joan is not merely a fanciful story; it is also a potent commentary on the nature of power and the limitations imposed by society. The idea that a woman could, even if fleetingly and under false pretenses, occupy the highest seat of ecclesiastical authority resonated deeply with later generations. During periods of reform and when popular discontent with entrenched Church practices reached a fever pitch, the narrative served as both a rallying cry for change and a symbolic assertion of gendered potential.

In the realms of art and literature, the image of Pope Joan has been both endlessly mutable and perennially fascinating. Renaissance playwrights, novelists, painters, and even composers found in her story a canvas on which they could project themes of tragic ambition, hidden courage, and the fierce struggle against societal constraints. Depictions range from portrayals of a deeply sympathetic heroine—a brilliant, oppressed woman forced to don the armor of male authority—to cautionary illustrations of the perils that arise when ambition, divorced from morality, spirals into chaos. Even if her historical existence remains unsubstantiated, her image has secured a lasting place in the collective imagination. This artistic legacy transformed Pope Joan from a mere scholarly curiosity into a living symbol—a figure whose very ambiguity invites us to question the nature of truth, the reliability of the historical record, and the intricate dance between myth and power.

At the core of the enduring debate surrounding Pope Joan lies a profound interplay between myth and institutional legitimacy. Although the story may not withstand rigorous historical scrutiny, its persistence speaks to an innate human fascination with challenging the status quo. In medieval society, when the Church loomed large over every aspect of life, the notion that its zenith might have been occupied—even temporarily—by a woman struck a resonant, if unsettling, chord. It not only allowed skeptics to question the sanctity of established traditions but also served as a vessel for ideas about the transformative potential of female authority—a challenge to the patriarchal order that continues to inspire debate even today.

Modern scholarly assessments largely dismiss the literal reality of a female pope, yet they acknowledge that the Pope Joan narrative holds an undeniable cultural and historiographical allure. It encourages us to reflect not just on the storied past of the medieval Church but on the broader processes through which legends are born, nurtured, and transformed. The tale interrogates how myths can both mirror and mold public perceptions of power and gender, forcing us to confront the ways history is recorded and remembered. Even if the historical Pope Joan is nothing more than a clever fabrication—a myth spun from the threads of dissent and disillusionment—her legend remains a provocative reminder of the capacity for human creativity to challenge the boundaries of accepted truth.

Ultimately, Pope Joan's saga resonates as a timeless confrontation between the latent potential for greatness and the harsh realities of cultural repression. It is a story oscillating between the awe-inspiring and the cautionary, between the yearning to transcend societal limits and the grim consequences of defying entrenched power. Her narrative, with all its evocative twists and heartrending climax, endures as both a warning and an inspirational rousing call to celebrate individual courage in the face of overwhelming odds, even if that celebration must take the form of myth. While the legend of Pope Joan may be fiction, its very existence and resonance throughout history illuminates the profound anxieties and critiques surrounding the Papacy's exercise of power—anxieties that often mirrored the very real moral failings and political abuses that the subsequent chapters of this book will explore.

In our modern era, where debates about gender, tradition, and authority continue to shape our cultural landscape, the enigma of Pope Joan remains as vibrant as ever. Her story invites us to peel back the layers of time, to interrogate the complexities of historical memory, and to embrace the enduring mystery at the crossroads of legend and reality. Though historical evidence for her existence may be as elusive as the shifting shadows in an ancient cloister, the spirit of her legend—one of defiant bravery and subversive elegance—continues to whisper across the centuries, challenging us to question the established order and to imagine a world unbound by the strictures of the past.

Chapter Two

The Cadaver Trial – Pope Stephen VI (896–897)

Late in the 9th century, Rome—a city scarred by centuries of political ruptures and bitter factional disputes—found itself in a turbulent era where divine authority clashed with the ambitions of mortal men. The decline of the Carolingian dynasty had left the Eternal City vulnerable, its streets echoing with the footsteps of opportunistic nobles, ambitious clerics, and foreign powers all vying for control. Amid this chaos, the papacy, once a beacon of spiritual guidance, was increasingly reduced to a pawn in a dangerous game of power politics. Behind the hallowed marble facades of basilicas and the ancient ceremonies of worship, there simmered relentless intrigues and treacherous alliances that would soon set in motion events destined to shake the very foundations of the Church.

In this volatile milieu, Pope Stephen VI emerged as a man driven not by the call of divine service but by personal vendetta and a desperate need to reassert control over an institution under siege from every side. His reign could be seen as both a symptom and a cause of the era's decadence, where loyalty was often sacrificed at the altar of ambition. At the heart of Stephen VI's ire lay Pope Formosus, a controversial predecessor whose ascent to power had been marked by dramatic alliances and contentious decisions. Formosus, whose papacy navigated turbulent relations with secular rulers and influential Roman factions, had dared to align himself with forces many considered inimical to the Church's sanctity. His crowning of Emperor Arnulf of Carinthia was not merely a gesture of imperial support but a strategic maneuver that, while bolstering his political influence, roused fierce opposition among Rome's aristocracy. This alliance, viewed by many as a betrayal of spiritual principles, set the stage for a more profound, more personal grudge that would soon transcend the boundaries of mortal life.

Determined to obliterate any memory of Formosus' alleged transgressions, Pope Stephen VI embarked on a course that remains one of the darkest episodes in ecclesiastical history. In an act of macabre theatricality that blurred the lines between justice and vengeance, he ordered the exhumation of Formosus' corpse. The desecrated remains of the former pontiff were not left to rest in peace but were instead dragged from their solemn interment to a makeshift court. In a spectacle that stunned both the clergy and the laity, the corpse was forced to occupy a symbolic throne as if it could still deliberate and speak, its silent form serving as a canvas for accusations that ranged from liturgical aberrations to outright crimes against the Church. The Cadaver Synod, as this grotesque trial came to be known, vividly illustrated a moment when the institutions of the Church were beset by the basest human impulses—vindictiveness and the lust for power taking precedence over spiritual sanctity.

Nevertheless, the spectacle was not only about erasing a political rival; it was a brilliantly executed piece of symbolic warfare. In the medieval mindset, the body and its posthumous treatment carried profound significance. To subject a corpse to judicial proceedings was to declare that even in death, Formosus' purported sins demanded penance. Such an act was designed to shock the collective conscience of the faithful and to delegitimize an entire faction that had once rallied behind the deceased pontiff. The grotesque ritual—complete with the recitation of accusations, the symbolic stripping of papal vestments, and the final decreeing of guilt—was a deliberate inversion of the natural order. By turning the solemn ritual of judgment into an affront to decency, Stephen VI sought to transform the memory of Formosus into a warning: a cautionary tale of ambition run amok, a stark demonstration that the sacred could be subverted by the ambitions of those unworthy of divine trust.

However, the Cadaver Synod served as a mirror, holding up to a much broader societal decay. It exposed the inherent vulnerability of an institution that had, over time, allowed itself to be hijacked by political machinations. Rome was a city of paradoxes—a place where the eternal spirit of Christianity clashed with the ephemeral passions of its human custodians. The spectacle of the dead pope on trial resonated deeply with a populace already disillusioned by a series of leadership crises and power struggles. For many, the event symbolized the breakdown of a moral and spiritual order that many had assumed unassailable for centuries. The longstanding tradition that the papal office was divinely ordained and thus insulated from mortal faults was shattered by a display of brutality that left an indelible scar on the collective memory of Christendom.

In the aftermath of the Synod, the political fallout was swift and severe. The public outrage was not confined to the corridors of the Vatican—it spilled into the streets of Rome and beyond, as citizens and clerics alike struggled to reconcile their reverence for the divine with the unseemly machinations that had just unfolded. Pope Stephen VI's brief reign, marked by cruelty and paranoia, ended as precipitously as it had begun; he himself fell victim to the tides of retribution. Imprisoned and ultimately strangled within the very walls he had sought so desperately to control, his demise served as a grim epilogue to a reign defined by its disregard for sacred tradition.

Nevertheless, even in the ruins of this scandal, the Church was not content to simply erase the stain of the past. Recognizing the profound damage inflicted upon its reputation, subsequent popes embarked on an ambitious project of rehabilitation and reform. Leaders such as Pope Theodore II and Pope John IX undertook the arduous task of restoring the dignity of the papacy by nullifying the judgments rendered at the Cadaver Synod. Through legal and theological means, they sought to reinstate the decisions made during Formosus' lifetime and reclaim the narrative from the clutches of factional vendetta. This period of reflection and reformation marked a turning point, as the Church began to understand that its spiritual authority could not coexist with the corruptions of temporal ambition.

Beyond the institutional reforms, the Cadaver Synod left a cultural legacy that has resonated through the ages. Scholars, theologians, and historians have long debated the symbolism embedded in that ghastly trial. Was it simply an aberration, a moment of unbridled cruelty by a desperate pope, or did it reveal deeper structural flaws in the medieval understanding of justice? In the dim light of historical hindsight, the Synod emerges as a powerful allegory for the dangers inherent in mixing divine office with secular ambition. The idea that a body – long dead and unresponsive – could be forced to stand trial represents, on one level, an indictment of the perversion of sacred practices. It forces modern observers to confront uncomfortable questions about the nature of power, the limits of authority, and the enduring tension between the spiritual and the temporal.

This legacy, far from being consigned to a footnote in ecclesiastical history, has continued to inform debates about the separation of Church and state, the role of religious institutions in political life, and the importance of maintaining moral integrity amid the temptations of power. The moral and theological lessons of the Cadaver Synod resonate in contemporary discussions about institutional ethics and leadership accountability. In many ways, the reverberations of that dark chapter in Rome's history serve as a timeless admonition—reminding each generation that the true strength of any institution lies not in its capacity for exerting control but in its commitment to principles that transcend the fleeting ambitions of men.

In reflecting on the Cadaver Synod, one cannot help but consider the broader human implications of such a spectacle. The visceral horror of subjecting a fallen leader to posthumous judgment speaks not only to the depths of political savagery but also to the profound complexities of reconciliation and regret. How does society come to terms with such a violation of the sacred? How do communities rebuild trust in an institution that has, even if momentarily, succumbed to the basest aspects of human ambition? For many, the Synod is a stark reminder that the search for power, when left unchecked, can easily overshadow a commitment to justice and mercy. It is an enduring lesson in the importance of tempering authority with humility—a theme that resonates as strongly today as it did in the turbulent corridors of medieval Rome.

This narrative of ambition, betrayal, and eventual reform reveals the Cadaver Synod not as an isolated horror of medieval politics but as a symbol of the eternal struggle between the divine and the profane. Its memory spurred a series of reforms aimed at disentangling spiritual leadership from the corrosive influences of political scheming. The painful process of undoing the wrongs of the past was not undertaken lightly; it involved a meticulous reordering of ecclesiastical law and a sincere effort to return to the core values that had once defined the papacy. The legacy of Formosus, once tarnished by the spectral proceedings of a deadly tribunal, was slowly restored—not as a testament to political expediency but as a symbol of enduring faith and the possibility of redemption.

In the complex interplay between divine mandate and human ambition, the story of the Cadaver Synod continues to fascinate and repel in equal measure. It is a narrative that challenges our perceptions of justice and authority, urging us to confront the often-painful intersection where the sacred meets the secular. As we sift through the annals of history, this episode is a grim reminder that history is not a static record of immutable truths but a dynamic, evolving discourse—a dialogue between the past and the present in which every generation must decide which voices will define its future. The echoes of that infamous trial remind us that even in the most hallowed halls, the struggle for truth and integrity is never truly resolved.

Ultimately, the enduring relevance of the Cadaver Synod lies in its bold, unyielding interrogation of power itself. It compels us to recognize that the institutions we hold sacred are not impervious to corruption and that vigilance, accountability, and an unwavering commitment to justice must guide our understanding of authority. In contemplating the tragic fate of Pope Formosus and the descent of his successors into moral ambiguity, we are invited to reflect on our own time—on how modern institutions balance power with principle and how the lessons of the past can inform a more just and equitable future. This timeless admonition serves as both a warning and an inspiration, urging us to remember that true leadership is not measured by the display of authority but by the compassion and integrity with which it is exercised.

In this narrative of ambition, betrayal, and eventual reform, the Cadaver Synod emerges not as an isolated horror of medieval politics but as a symbol of the eternal struggle between the divine and the profane. It stands as a somber testament to the perils of unchecked ambition—a resonance that continues to echo through centuries of ecclesiastical reflection and scholarly debate. Furthermore, though

ALLEN SCHERY

the events of that fateful period remain confined to the pages of history, their lessons are as pertinent today as they were in the turbulent corridors of 9th-century Rome, calling each generation to honor the sacred by safeguarding the integrity of both their institutions and their souls.

Chapter Three

The Avignon Papacy and the Western Schism: A Divided Throne.

The Renaissance Papacy, with its worldly ambitions and often scandalous popes, did not emerge in a vacuum. It was, in many ways, a reaction to, and a continuation of, a profound crisis that had gripped the papacy in the preceding centuries: the Avignon Papacy and the subsequent Western Schism. This period fundamentally challenged the very notion of a unified spiritual authority and laid bare the immense pressures of political power and human fallibility on the Chair of St. Peter. It demonstrated a different kind of "shadow" – not just personal moral failing, but a deep institutional crisis born from the Church's entanglement with secular forces.

The roots of the Avignon Papacy trace back to the early 14th century, stemming from growing tensions between the French monarchy and the papacy, specifically the fierce power struggle between

King Philip IV of France and Pope Boniface VIII. Philip asserted the supremacy of royal power over ecclesiastical authority, leading to open conflict. After Boniface's death and the brief pontificate of Benedict XI, a Frenchman, Raymond Bertrand de Got, was elected pope in 1305, taking the name Clement V. Under intense pressure from Philip IV, and citing political instability and dangers in Rome, Clement V made the controversial decision in 1309 to relocate the papal court from Rome to Avignon, a city then on the southeastern border of France. What was initially intended as a temporary move stretched into nearly 70 years, with six successive popes, all French, reigning from Avignon.

This long absence from Rome, often referred to by its critics as the "Babylonian Captivity of the Papacy" (a direct parallel drawn to the biblical exile of the Jews), profoundly damaged the papacy's prestige and universality. Rome, the traditional seat of St. Peter and the apostolic heart of the Church, fell into disrepair and chaos, further fueling calls for the pope's return. The Avignon popes, while maintaining an increasingly sophisticated and powerful administrative machinery of the Church, were widely perceived as subservient to the French crown, leading to accusations of corruption, excessive fiscal demands, and undue French influence. They expanded the system of papal taxation and benefice reservation, creating a well-oiled financial machine, but one that often prioritized revenue over spiritual needs, making the papacy seem more like a secular treasury than a spiritual beacon. European powers outside of France, such as England and the Holy Roman Empire, grew deeply suspicious of papal motives, viewing the Church leadership through a lens of national interest rather than universal spiritual guidance. This period was a direct manifestation of the papacy's deep entanglement with secular politics, showing how even the spiritual head of Christendom could become a pawn in the game of nations, thereby eroding the perception of its divine independence.

The crisis escalated dramatically in 1377, when Pope Gregory XI finally returned the papacy to Rome, largely due to the impassioned and persuasive efforts of St. Catherine of Siena, a mystic who passionately argued for the pope's return as a spiritual necessity for the Church. However, Gregory XI died shortly after, and the subsequent papal election in 1378 was fraught with unprecedented tension and violence. Roman citizens, desperate to keep the papacy in their city and fearing the election of another French pope who might return to Avignon, rioted and exerted immense pressure on the cardinals gathered in conclave. Under perceived duress, the cardinals elected Urban VI, an Italian. Urban VI quickly alienated many cardinals with his abrasive manner, fiery temper, and radical reformist zeal, threatening to curb their power and privileges. This led a powerful faction of French cardinals, soon joined by others, to declare his election invalid due to the coercion they had faced, claiming their votes were cast out of fear for their lives.

These dissenting cardinals then retreated from Rome and, in September 1378, elected their own pope, Clement VII, a Frenchman, who re-established a papal court in Avignon. This catastrophic event marked the beginning of the Western Schism, a period of nearly 40 years where two (and at one point, three) legitimate lines of popes simultaneously claimed authority over the Catholic Church. Europe was immediately and painfully divided along political and national lines, with kingdoms recognizing different pontiffs based on their existing alliances and geopolitical interests. France, Scotland, Castile (Spain), and parts of Italy largely supported the Avignon line, while England, the Holy Roman Empire (Germany), and other Italian states backed the Roman pope. Universities, religious orders, and even individual families were tragically split in their loyalties.

The Western Schism plunged Christendom into spiritual and institutional chaos, representing a profound "shadow" that obscured the Church's divine mission. With no clear single head of the Church, questions of legitimacy, the validity of sacraments performed by clergy ordained by rival popes, and ultimately, individual salvation became agonizingly complex for ordinary believers and theologians alike. Which pope was true? Which sacraments were valid? Whom should bishops obey? The very fabric of ecclesiastical order seemed to unravel. Popes excommunicated each other, denouncing their rivals as anti-popes or heretics, further confusing the faithful and eroding trust in the institution.

Attempts to resolve the crisis through diplomacy or the resignation of both popes proved futile, as neither claimant was willing to cede his perceived rightful authority. This led to the extraordinary measure of convening ecumenical councils. The Council of Pisa in 1409 attempted to resolve the impasse by unilaterally deposing both existing popes (Gregory XII in Rome and Benedict XIII in Avignon) and electing a new one, Alexander V. However, this desperate move only exacerbated the schism, as neither of the original popes recognized the council's authority, resulting in a bewildering situation with three competing popes.

The resolution finally came at the much larger and more authoritative Council of Constance (1414-1418). This council, backed by the Holy Roman Emperor Sigismund and involving representatives from across Europe, successfully asserted its power over the reigning pontiffs. Through a combination of diplomatic pressure, theological argument, and sheer political will, the council managed to depose the claimant in Pisa, accept the resignation of the Roman pope, and isolate the Avignon pope (who stubbornly refused to resign). In 1417, the Council of Constance elected Pope Martin V, effectively reuniting the papacy in Rome and ending the devastating schism.

This momentous achievement came at a cost, however: the Council of Constance also asserted the supremacy of ecumenical councils over the pope in certain matters—a doctrine known as conciliarism—which would continue to challenge absolute papal authority for decades to come, leaving a lasting impact on how future popes would govern.

The Avignon Papacy and the Western Schism represent a profound and traumatic "shadow" in papal history. They showcase how internal divisions, intense political pressures, and the unyielding nature of human ambition could tear at the very fabric of an institution claiming divine mandate. The prolonged absence from Rome, the accusations of French subservience, the fiscal abuses, and the scandal of multiple popes not only deeply damaged the papacy's moral standing but also profoundly eroded the spiritual unity of Christendom. While the schism was eventually healed, it left an indelible mark on the Church, contributing to a growing demand for fundamental, institutional reform that, within a century, would explode into the Protestant Reformation. The memory of a divided papacy would serve as a stark reminder of the perils of worldly entanglement and the constant need for spiritual purity within the Church's highest office.

Chapter Four

Pope Sergius III
(904-911)

I n the twilight of early medieval Rome—a period marked by political volatility, the decline of ancient virtues, and the relentless
encroachment of secular ambition upon the sacred—Pope Sergius
III emerges as one of history's most controversial and complex figures. Born around 860 into a venerable Roman aristocratic family,
his early years were ensconced in a world where privilege was insep-
arable from political maneuvering. From an early age, Sergius ab-
sorbed the dual lessons of classical learning and the ruthless practices
of aristocratic diplomacy. His upbringing, characterized by lavish
ceremonies, rigorous study of religious dogma, and an intimate ac-
quaintance with the intrigues of noble courts, set the stage for his
later turbulent ascent into ecclesiastical power. In an era later known
as the "saeculum obscurum" or the dark age of the papacy, when the
boundaries between sacred duty and worldly ambition were increasingly blurred, Sergius's life trajectory promised profound influence

and ignoble scandal. His destiny, as recorded in fragmented manuscripts and later historical accounts, would become emblematic of an epoch when spiritual authority was subverted by the ambitions of powerful families and the exigencies of brutal political contests.

The early tenth century in Italy was a maelstrom of rivalry and factional strife that redefined the nature of leadership within the Church. The remnants of imperial glory had given way to a landscape where various aristocratic families—most notably the Tusculani, under the formidable Theophylact I of Tusculum—jockeyed for supremacy. In this fractious environment, the papacy transformed from a purely spiritual institution into a prize contested by ambitious clans. Power was won and lost through secret pacts, bloodshed, and shifting alliances, and ecclesiastical appointments were as much the product of political negotiation as they were of supposed divine selection. Against this backdrop, Sergius's rise cannot be understood merely as a sequence of religious milestones; rather, it was inseparably defined by the interplay of noble patronage, mendacious electoral practices, and the inexorable drive of personal ambition. This atmosphere of corruption and intrigue undermined the traditional sanctity of the papal office and provided fertile ground for personal scandals that would mar Sergius's reputation for generations.

Sergius's formal journey into the inner circles of the Church began with his ordination under Pope Marinus I and subsequent elevation to the diaconate by Pope Stephen V. Recognizing his administrative promise, Pope Formosus, whose turbulent reign was itself a prelude to later institutional decay, appointed him Bishop of Caere (modern Cerveteri) in 893. Although his appointment temporarily removed him from the epicenter of Roman politics, it was also instrumental in embedding him within a vast network of clerics and lay patrons. In this role, he cultivated connections that would later prove essential for his bid to ascend to the papacy. His early ecclesiastical formation was marked by an amalgamation of piety and pragmatism—a combination enabling and complicating his subsequent political maneuvering. In Rome's cloisters and lecture halls, he was schooled in theology and liturgy and the subtleties of power politics. These experiences instilled in him a keen understanding that the Church's spiritual mission was, during these turbulent times, inextricably linked with the ambitions and betrayals characteristic of the Roman aristocracy.

However, the path to power was seldom straightforward in a landscape dominated by constant back-and-forth struggles for supremacy. Sergius's ascent to the papal throne was emblematic of a process rife with contested elections, sudden exiles, and violent reassertions—all against a backdrop of factional discord. In 898, his initial election as pope ignited fierce opposition from rival factions and opened the door to interference by imperial interests, notably those aligned with Emperor Lambert. The resulting power vacuum forced him temporarily into exile at Caere, serving both as a retreat from immediate danger and as a period that further hardened his resolve. This interregnum, punctuated by the uncertainties of shifting allegiances and clandestine negotiations, set the stage for his dramatic return. On January 29, 904, with the decisive backing of Theophylact I—a patriarch of the powerful Tusculani family, Sergius reemerged in Rome, his return marked by ruthless political maneuvering. In an episode that would forever stain his legacy, he deposed Antipope Christopher and Pope Leo V, an overt demonstration of noble factions' lengths to secure ecclesiastical power. This violent and calculated accession underscored not only the tenuous nature of papal legitimacy during this era but also the extent to which the ambitions of aristocratic elites were manipulating the sacred office.

Once installed as the pontiff, Sergius III inherited a Church deeply divided by internal strife and external corruption. Among his most notorious actions was his association with the infamous Cadaver Synod—a macabre tribunal held to condemn his predecessor, Pope Formosus, posthumously. Although Sergius's direct involvement is debated among historians, his reign provided fertile ground for such unprecedented events, emblematic of a broader strategy to delegitimize rival factions and consolidate his power. By convening synods that revisited and, in some cases, nullified decisions of earlier pontifical decrees, Sergius sought to reshape the Church's internal structures to favor the political interests of his noble backers. These assemblies, conducted with an atmosphere of palpable tension and underlying brutality, not only served to cast doubts on established ecclesiastical traditions but also deepened existing fissures among the clergy. Meanwhile, efforts to restore the physical structure, such as the renovation of the Lateran Basilica, damaged by years of conflict and neglect, were undertaken to project an image of renewal, even as the moral foundation of the papacy continued to crumble under the weight of scandal.

Integral to the enduring legacy of Pope Sergius III are the personal scandals that have colored his historical reputation as much as, if not more than, his political achievements. Among the most enduring controversies is the alleged liaison with Marozia, a formidable and ambitious daughter of Theophylact I. The nature of their relationship, whether it was genuine or the concoction of politically motivated enemies, underscores the pervasive influence of noble families on the papacy during the "saeculum obscurum." Allegations persist that this relationship produced an illegitimate son who later ascended to the papacy as John XI, further complicating the already murky distinctions between legitimate lineage and the exercise of power. The chroniclers of the time, whose works were often steeped in moral judgment, recorded these personal transgressions in detail, and later historians have debated the extent to which such scandals were amplified by those intent on discrediting an already embattled institution. Regardless of their precise veracity, these allegations are a potent symbol of the era's moral decay and the dangers inherent when worldly desires compromise spiritual authority.

Beyond the internal corridors of Rome, the policies and decisions of Pope Sergius III had significant repercussions on the broader stage of international diplomacy. One of the more contentious episodes of his pontificate was his refusal to crown Berengar I as the Holy Roman Emperor. This decision reverberated widely among both Italian nobility and external powers. The act was not merely a defiant gesture on the part of the papacy; it was a calculated political move that underscored the tension between maintaining an independent spiritual authority and succumbing to the demands of temporal rulers. In parallel, Sergius's support for specific policies promoted by Byzantine Emperor Leo VI—particularly those addressing the intricacies of marital legitimacy and royal succession—illustrated the delicate balancing act required to navigate the competing influences of Western and Eastern Christendom. Such decisions reveal a papacy caught between doctrinal conservatism and the pragmatic needs of survival in a world where shifting alliances could decide the fate of entire regions. While perhaps effective in the short term, these maneuvers contributed to long-lasting tensions that would eventually culminate in further schisms and reforms within the Church.

The institutional impact of Sergius III's reign is felt in the annals of papal history and the evolving narrative of Church reform. His tenure, marked by overt manipulation and subtle subversion of ecclesiastical norms, led to widespread disillusionment among clergy and laity alike. The policies enacted during his pontificate—such as the repeated reconvening of synods to challenge the legitimacy of previous appointments—eroded trust in the sanctity of papal succession. As a result, his rule became a catalyst for subsequent reform movements that sought to reclaim the moral authority and spiritual purity once associated with the papacy. In retrospect, while successfully consolidating power for his noble allies temporarily, the actions taken under his aegis ultimately paved the way for a broader reckoning within the Church. They highlighted the perilous consequences of allowing temporal ambitions to override genuine spiritual commitment. They set a precedent for the internal conflicts that would shape the ecclesiastical reforms of later centuries.

Scholars over the years have engaged in fierce debate regarding the true legacy of Pope Sergius III. Early chroniclers, who were contemporaneous with the events they described, were often unflinching in their condemnation of his rule—depicting him as a leader driven solely by ambition, indulgence, and a desire for personal gain. Modern historians, however, tend to offer a more nuanced assessment, arguing that his actions must be understood within a society where the lines between sacred duty and political pragmatism are profoundly blurred. Some contemporary analyses suggest that while his failings cannot be denied, his policies were also a product of an environment in which every aspiring leader was compelled to engage in practices that, by modern standards, would be considered corrupt. This reassessment underscores the complexity of judging historical figures by today's moral standards and highlights the tension between historical context and retrospective ethical evaluation.

Finally, when reflecting on the long-term lessons gleaned from the tumultuous pontificate of Pope Sergius III, one is confronted with enduring questions about the nature of power, leadership, and human frailty. His reign encapsulates the paradox that even an office as hallowed as the papacy is not immune to the corrupting influence of ambition. Sergius's life—replete with dramatic episodes of violent power grabs, intricate political alliances, and deeply personal scandals—mirrors modern institutions, illustrating the perennial challenge of balancing idealism with pragmatism. In his life, we see a vivid illustration of how personal ambition, when interwoven with the complex fabric of political forces, can lead to a legacy that is as much about moral compromise as it is about institutional transformation. His narrative compels us to reflect on the fundamental vulnerability of all human systems, where the quest for glory and control often comes at the price of spiritual integrity.

Chapter Five

Pope John XII & Pope Benedict IX (955–1048)

The medieval world was a crucible of ambition and dynastic intrigue—a time when personal vice and corruption frequently pierced the thin veneer of sanctity. In an era when the papacy was meant to be the paragon of spiritual virtue, even its highest officers became instruments of human desire and relentless ambition. The eternal struggle between sacred duty and worldly temptation left deep scars on the Church's legacy and altered the notion of divine authority. Chroniclers of the age, inscribing their observations in terse Latin phrases and ornate illuminated manuscripts, witnessed an institution that was fated to be a beacon of moral guidance but became mired in factional intrigue and personal debauchery.

Political turbulence was rife throughout medieval Europe. The slow decay of long-established dynasties, combined with the rise of powerful local families and a burgeoning mercantile class, set sweeping economic and social changes into motion. In this environment, even technological advances—a precursor to the printing press—amplified the dissemination of ideas once confined to secluded monastic quarters. Pamphlets, handwritten tracts, and satirical broadsheets began circulating among the literate as a growing public appetite for knowledge and gossip confronted the old regime of unquestioned authority. Reformers and critics alike seized upon every sign of papal excess, using each transgression as evidence that even the most hallowed office was vulnerable to the corrosive influence of human ambition.

Amid this volatile backdrop, two papacies stand out as emblematic of the larger crises of the age—those of Pope John XII and Pope Benedict IX. Their reigns, mired in scandal and marked by behavior that defied the solemn expectations of spiritual leadership, transformed the papal office into a commodity—a badge of honor to be traded among Rome's elite rather than a divine mantle entrusted only to the worthy. In these turbulent decades, the Church's moral authority started to crumble, and its internal fissures became increasingly exposed to a restless public longing for reform.

When Pope John XII ascended the papal throne at an exceedingly young age, there were initial expectations of wisdom and humility befitting one chosen by divine providence. However, in a stunning divergence from these ideals, contemporary accounts—etched in biting satire and recorded in the private letters of monastic scribes—depicted a man whose conduct starkly contrasts the sacred mandate of his office. Rather than serving as a humble shepherd, John XII quickly devolved into a figure synonymous with scandal: his ostentatious feasts, his blatant disregard for liturgical decorum, and his licentious behavior within the confines of his household painted a portrait of a papacy besieged by carnal indulgence. Every sumptuous banquet and every profane jest became fodder for chroniclers who, despite potential bias from bitter political adversaries, ensured that his misdeeds were immortalized as a monumental affront to divine expectation.

Born Theophylactus of Tusculum around 1012 into one of Rome's most influential aristocratic families, he was immersed from early childhood in an environment where the worlds of secular power and ecclesiastical influence converged. The Tusculani had long wielded considerable wealth and political influence, using carefully cultivated relationships to shape papal elections and sway church policies. In such a milieu, education was not confined solely to the classical studies of literature and philosophy but also involved the pragmatic—and often ruthless—lessons of negotiation and high-stakes patronage. For young Theophylactus, these early influences helped forge a brilliant and contentious character. In October 1032, at the exceptionally young age of 18, he was chosen to lead the Church—a record-setting ascension that shocked contemporary observers and symbolized the gradual secularization of a role once thought exclusively divine.

At this juncture, early 11th-century Rome was a city defined by relentless power struggles and delicate alliances. The papacy, which had formerly been regarded as a purely sacred institution, became subject to the competing ambitions of aristocratic families and secular lords. Influential figures—like Count Alberic III of Tusculum—used their sway over local politics to ensure that the bishopric and papal office could serve as instruments of family prestige and control. In this volatile context, the deliberate choice of an 18-year-old to serve as pope may seem radical, yet it reflected the prevailing realities of the time: the conflation of political necessity with spiritual responsibility. To many contemporaries, his ascension was both an emblem of youthful promise and a portent of the profound changes that were reshaping ecclesiastical authority.

Assuming the papal office amid such turbulence, Benedict IX inherited an institution besieged by conflicting interests. His youthful vigor, initially hailed as a signal of renewal, rapidly provoked heated debates over his suitability for a role that demanded intellectual maturity and a profound sense of moral duty. Critics questioned whether he possessed the requisite gravitas to manage an institution burdened by centuries of tradition. At the same time, his supporters argued that such energy might be precisely what a stagnant system needed. Early chroniclers, who wrote with equal admiration and moral indignation, described his court as a glittering assembly of aristocrats, ambitious clerics, and influential courtiers. Lavish banquets, exuberant celebrations, and impulsive administrative decisions soon emerged as hallmarks of his reign—characteristics that starkly contrasted with the piety and moderation traditionally expected of a spiritual leader.

Nevertheless, modern historians carefully interpret these early accounts with a critical eye. Many of the narratives about Benedict IX were composed by later reformers intending to expose the corruption they perceived within the Church; as such, some details have been amplified in the service of moral critique. While it is indisputable that his behavior deviated from normative clerical decorum, the more sensational descriptions must be balanced against the recognized political complexities of his time. Thus, while his court was undoubtedly marked by extravagance and irregular administration, interpretations of his debaucheries are now tempered by contemporary scholarship, emphasizing the need to separate factual events from later evaluative embellishments.

During his initial reign—from 1032 to 1044—Benedict IX's papacy was dogged by mounting internal struggles and public controversies. His government, primarily driven by the customary practices of nepotism and family favoritism, increasingly came under fire as factions within the Roman elite began to contest his authority. While such practices were not unusual at the time, they progressively undermined the moral prestige of the papal office. As internal divisions became more pronounced, political pressures reached a fever pitch, and by 1044, Benedict IX found himself forced into exile. In a dramatic and unprecedented turn, he resigned from the papacy. Later accounts—inflected with both disbelief and moral outrage—suggest that he transferred the office to his godfather, Giovanni Graziano, who became Pope Gregory VI in May 1045. This act, whether viewed as a resignation under duress or as a calculated political maneuver, underscored the extent to which the integrity of the papal institution had been compromised in that era.

Nevertheless, Benedict IX was not one to relinquish ambition lightly. In a stunning demonstration of resilience, he managed a short-lived comeback later in 1045, only to be deposed once again and to resume a final tenure from 1047 to 1048. These three non-consecutive reigns, all unfolding within 16 years, constitute a phenomenon unique in the annals of papal history. They epitomize a period during which the sacred office was rendered vulnerable not only to external political manipulations but also to internal factional disputes and the turbulent aspirations of a single leader. His repeated depositions and restorations became a potent symbol of an institutional crisis, reflecting how the boundaries between spiritual authority and worldly ambition had grown perilously indistinct.

The broader implications of his reign extend well beyond the immediate political turbulence of medieval Rome. The controversies and excesses that marked Benedict IX's papacy provided fertile ground for those later committed to institutional reform. When subsequent popes—most notably Pope Gregory VII—set about restoring a sense of moral and organizational integrity to the Church, they often cited the abuses of Benedict IX's era as clear evidence of the need for sweeping changes. The Gregorian reforms, which emerged in the latter part of the 11th century, were in many ways a direct response to the pervasive corruption that his tumultuous career had exposed, including practices such as simony and nepotism. Seen in this light, his troubled reign can be interpreted not merely as an episode of scandal but as a catalyst—a disruptive force that spurred a long-overdue evolution in the governance of the Church.

In the realm of cultural memory, the name of Pope Benedict IX has continued to resonate long after he departed from power. Over the centuries, his story has inspired many artistic and literary works exploring the human dimensions of ambition and the pitfalls of unchecked authority. From medieval chronicles to modern historical novels and documentaries, his life has been reimagined and reinterpreted through many different lenses. These creative renditions, whether in subtle allegory or bold dramatization, reflect the complex interplay between spiritual ideals and the baser impulses associated with temporal power. In this way, his enduring legacy is not merely one of scandal but also of profound historical significance—a subject of study that continues to provoke debate and inspire inquiry.

Alongside these cultural illustrations is the modern academic dialogue that has revisited the narrative of Benedict IX in depth. Scholars have long debated the extent to which later accounts overstate his personal excesses and moral failings, striving instead to construct a picture as nuanced as the historical record permits. Detailed examinations of surviving primary sources reveal the dual nature of his career: on the one hand, an 18-year-old catapulted into a role of immense responsibility in a time of great uncertainty; on the other hand, a figure whose repeated imprisonments and restorations underline the inherent instability wrought by the mingling of familial politics with sacred office. Such discussions compel modern readers to engage with his story on multiple levels—analyzing the facts of his reign and the methodologies by which history is recorded, interpreted, and sometimes mythologized.

Modern interdisciplinary studies have further enriched our understanding of his tumultuous period. Scholars from fields as diverse as political science, sociology, art history, and literary studies have drawn upon his life to elaborate on broader themes such as institutional decay, moral responsibility, and the mechanisms of power. Conferences and journal articles have dissected the paradox of his early ascension and the subsequent rapid reversals of fortune, drawing parallels with contemporary discussions on governance and ethical leadership. In this way, the legacy of Pope Benedict IX transcends its medieval origins, offering lessons that remain strikingly relevant to the challenges of leadership in various modern contexts.

Adding to the academic richness, modern self-publishing platforms and digital archives enable a more interactive form of historical scholarship. Today's academic works often include visual aids—such as annotated timelines, maps of medieval Rome, and reproduced excerpts of primary source documents—to complement extensive prose narratives. Such elements help situate Benedict IX's controversial reign within its socio-political and cultural context, allowing readers to visualize how power and tradition intersected in a dramatically changing world. These enhancements not only deepen the reader's engagement but also serve to underscore the multifaceted nature of historical inquiry.

The story of Pope Benedict IX also invites a reflective examination of leadership and institutional accountability in our era. His life challenges us to consider how youthful ambition, without a proper framework of accountability and ethical guidance, can lead to rapid and sometimes catastrophic upheaval—even in institutions regarded as sacred. For contemporary leaders in politics, academia, and business alike, his tumultuous career serves as a reminder of the importance of transparency, institutional checks and balances, and a commitment to core values. In an era where public trust is frequently tested by scandal and self-interest, the historical lessons drawn from his reign offer timeless insights into the necessity of reform and ethical stewardship.

Moreover, by comparing his career with those of later popes who managed to instill reform and reassert spiritual authority, readers gain a broader perspective on the evolution of Church governance. Whereas Benedict IX's reign is remembered for rapid changes in leadership and moral ambiguity, subsequent leaders ensured that the reforms initiated after his tenure laid the groundwork for a renewed Church that sought to restore the dignity of its sacred office and affirm its spiritual mission. This comparative approach heightens the historical contrast and provides a framework for understanding how crises, no matter how chaotic, can eventually catalyze positive transformation.

The corruption that emanated from the misuse of sacred authority resonated far beyond the cloistered halls of the Vatican. Economic pressures and a revived interest in classical learning had kindled a spirit of intellectual ferment that questioned every aspect of established power. The emerging mercantile class, ever hungry for information and influence, embraced this new wave of critical inquiry. Crowds gathered in public squares, where vocal dissent was expressed through revolutionary pamphlets and biting satires that cast the antics of John XII and Benedict IX in scathing relief. These printed and handwritten critiques underscored the erosion of papal credibility and served as early signals of a broader cultural transformation. This movement would eventually reshape the relationship between Church and state.

Eyewitness accounts add layers of poignant humanity to this historical tapestry. Personal letters from mid-ranking clerics lamented the "ruined visage of holiness" that had once been the hallmark of spiritual leadership, while ordinary parishioners recorded in their private diaries the slow disintegration of trust in an institution that had long been seen as the nexus between the divine and the mortal. In one particularly evocative account recovered from a monastic chronicle, a local priest described how the decline of papal virtue had transformed his sermons from calls to divine duty into mournful elegies for a lost moral order. In every whispered conversation and public declaration, the abuse of sacred authority by figures such as John XII and Benedict IX deepened a pervasive sense of betrayal. This sense of betrayal would fuel reformist zeal for many generations to come.

However, even as the corruption of the papal office reached its nadir, the Church displayed extraordinary resilience. The public outcry and growing intellectual unrest eventually catalyzed early reform movements. Ecclesiastical councils were convened, and stricter canonical measures were slowly implemented to purge the institution of the venal excesses that had come to define it. Drawing inspiration from ancient dogma and emerging humanistic ideals, reformers set about redefining what it meant to lead a spiritual community. Although at times clumsy and fraught with their own political compromises, the initial corrective measures laid the foundational groundwork for later, more systematic reforms such as the Gregorian Reforms and, eventually, the turbulent epochs of the Counter-Reformation.

The fighting spirit of reform was not confined solely to internal ecclesiastical debates; it seeped into the cultural and artistic expressions of the time. Illuminated manuscripts, frescoes, and even the earliest forms of printed literature began incorporating themes of rebirth and renewal, using allegory and satire to question the integrity of those who had so egregiously betrayed the sacred trust. Artists and writers, compelled to reflect on the states of their society and its leadership, frequently invoked the tales of John XII's excesses and Benedict IX's duplicity as powerful cautionary allegories. Over time, these narratives evolved into a collective myth that underscored the eternal struggle between the pursuit of temporal power and the aspiration to reach toward the divine—a struggle to recur throughout European history.

The measurable impact of these scandals on medieval politics cannot be overstated. Rival factions exploited these public debacles, using them as rallying cries in their broader campaigns to dismantle the centralized authority of the Church. Noble families, emboldened by the demonstrable faults of their spiritual superiors, formally challenged the centuries-old sanctity of papal decrees. The idea that a pope's actions could be scrutinized, satirized, and even challenged in the public arena was a radical departure from an age when the Divine Right had once protected the office from such mortal reproach. The debates kindled by these controversies would eventually yield new political structures—a gradual reordering of power that smoothed the transition from feudal loyalties to the emergence of the modern state.

It is within this expansive and evolving framework that the legacy of Pope John XII and Pope Benedict IX becomes especially resonant. While contributing to a period of profound institutional decay, their misrule also initiated a process of self-examination within the Church—a process that demanded accountability, encouraged introspection, and ultimately spurred a renaissance of reform-minded thought. Their lives and reigns transformed the medieval Church from an entity seemingly immune to criticism into one forced to reckon with its shortcomings. In this intricate interplay of vice and virtue, the scandalous episodes of papal excess served as both ignominy and impetus—a painful but necessary catalyst for systemic renewal.

In reflecting on these turbulent chapters, one is struck by the enduring impact that personal ambition and institutional corruption can have on the facade of sanctity. The abuses by John XII and Benedict IX raise uncomfortable questions about the nature of power and the vulnerability of even the most revered institutions to internal decay. Their stories compel us to consider how future generations will judge the actions of modern leaders who, like their medieval counterparts, are often caught in the irresistible currents of ambition, desire, and political intrigue. The historical record of these popes is a stark reminder that the purity of any revered institution must be vigilantly maintained through ongoing reform, transparency, and a relentless commitment to the highest ethical ideals.

Even as we examine the narratives of medieval misrule, it is important to acknowledge that the era was defined not solely by scandal but also by a profound capacity for transformation. The bitter lessons learned from the excesses of corrupted papacies galvanized a renewed sense of purpose among reformers and visionaries within the Church. From the ashes of the scandal, new ideals emerged**,** ones that placed a premium on accountability, moral rectitude, and the long-term integrity of spiritual leadership. These ideals would eventually crystallize into sweeping reforms that reshaped the Church and the broader contours of European society in the centuries to come.

In the grand narrative of history, the turbulent episodes of Pope John XII and Pope Benedict IX transcend mere scandal. They serve as timeless allegories for the perpetual conflict between human frailty and the aspiration toward the divine—a conflict that demands continuous vigilance and the willingness to sacrifice personal ambition for the greater good. Their reigns, replete with tragic errors and unintended catalysts for renewal, remind us that the journey toward a just and moral order is neither linear nor free of setbacks. Instead, it is a long, arduous struggle marked equally by moments of despair and the bright sparks of transformation.

Thus, even as recent generations recounted their misdeeds with indignation, these papacies continue to offer valuable lessons in the necessity of reform and the eternal vigilance required to secure true spiritual integrity. They stand not only as cautionary tales of unchecked ambition but also as symbols of an institution's remarkable ability to self-correct, adapt, and ultimately renew itself against all odds. Indeed, in every subsequent debate on governance, leadership, and ethical responsibility, the legacy of these medieval popes remains a resonant call for accountability that, over the centuries, has inspired reformers and common folk alike to demand that the light of divine integrity shine clearly in a world all too willing to be shadowed by personal gain.

Chapter Six
The Boniface & Urban Factors – Politics at the Heart of Medieval Rome (1294–1389)

P ower, ambition, and the delicate balance between spiritual authority and secular rule shaped the fate of medieval Europe. The papacy, once regarded as the supreme moral compass of Christendom, became increasingly entangled in the volatile political rivalries of kings, emperors, and aristocratic factions. As the Church strove to preserve its dominance amid shifting tides of governance, it morphed into both a fortress of divine authority and a battleground for earthly ambition. Few figures illustrate this conflict as vividly as Pope Boniface VIII and Pope Urban VI—two leaders whose reigns were marked by ideological struggles, bitter conflict, and legacies that would reverberate across centuries.

The political landscape of late medieval Europe was undergoing a profound transformation. The rise of powerful monarchies—fueled by the consolidation of territory and the emergence of centralized bureaucracies—challenged the Church's age-old claim to uncontested supremacy. Kings like Philip IV of France and others throughout Christendom began to resent what they viewed as an overreach of papal ambition into temporal affairs. The papacy, for its part, wasn't content to surrender its lofty claims. Determined to assert its primacy, the Church doubled down on its doctrinal declarations. This period witnessed fierce debates in royal courts, trenchant polemics in emerging literary pamphlets, and vigorous discussions among theologians about the proper limits of ecclesiastical authority. Such contests of power weren't simply abstract disputes; they profoundly affected the lives of millions, setting the stage for political revolution and deep institutional reform.

Pope Boniface VIII, whose pontificate spanned from 1294 to 1303, emerged as a man of uncompromising will and bold vision. His reign is particularly notable for his ambitious efforts to cement the Church's authority in the face of rising monarchical power. Boniface saw the papal office not simply as a spiritual guide but as the ultimate arbiter of all secular and divine matters. His issuance of the decree Unam Sanctam in 1302 was a watershed moment in medieval political thought. In that document, Boniface declared that salvation for every human being was predicated on absolute submission to papal authority. It wasn't a mere theological statement—it was a political manifesto intended to curb the growing ambitions of secular rulers and assert the papacy as the undisputed spiritual leader of Christendom, a claim meant to extend even to the most powerful kings.

However, Boniface's ideological declaration came at a time when monarchs were asserting their rights on the European stage. King Philip IV of France, known for his strategic prowess and determined ambition to strengthen royal authority, soon saw Boniface's expansive claims as a direct challenge to his sovereignty. The resulting confrontation was both bitter and dramatic. Philip, who deemed papal interference in matters of taxation and clerical appointments intolerable, led a campaign to curtail the papacy's influence over his kingdom. Tensions escalated to a head when, in the fateful events at Anagni in 1303, agents of the French crown stormed Boniface's residence and physically assaulted him. This singular moment—where divine authority met violent earthly resistance—became emblematic of shifting geopolitical realities and signaled that the papacy's hold over secular power was loosening.

The consequences of Boniface VIII's reign rippled far beyond the years of his pontificate. His unwavering commitment to defending ecclesiastical supremacy while initially raising the profile of the Church's doctrinal claims ultimately alienated significant segments of the clergy and the ruling elite—his confrontational stance set in motion a reordering of power relationships in Europe. Monarchs, having witnessed the vulnerabilities of an institution that once wielded the power to crown emperors and dictate the fate of nations, began to encroach more boldly upon the realms once sacrosanct to the Church. Boniface's vision of an absolute, divinely sanctioned papacy gave way under the pragmatic pressure of political realities—a reality in which ideological rigidity, when met with the force of modern statecraft, can weaken even the most formidable institutions.

In stark contrast to Boniface's defiant assertions stands the reign of Pope Urban VI, whose troubled tenure from 1378 to 1389 reveals the dangers of internal instability within the Church. Urban VI inherited an institution already rife with discord: factionalized loyalties, bitter rivalries between adherents of the Rome-based and Avignon-based papacies, and simmering discontent among the clergy. Rather than addressing these divisions with the measured diplomacy demanded, Urban's temperament and autocratic style deepened the institution's fissures. His reign soon descended into chaos as paranoia gripped him, and he launched sweeping purges against cardinals and clerics who were perceived as political threats. To secure his power, Urban resorted to ruthless measures—imprisoning, exiling, and even ordering the execution of those who challenged his rule. Consequently, his authoritarian governance catalyzed a deep crisis that further weakened the papacy and directly contributed to the eruption of the Western Schism.

The Western Schism was a dramatic rupture in the unity of Christendom. Rival claimants to the papal throne emerged rapidly, and every European ruler was forced to declare allegiance to one faction or the other. What had once been a singular, unifying institution was now fractured—a mosaic of competing authorities, each asserting their divine mandate. This schism magnified the already significant divisions within the Church and led to widespread political and spiritual uncertainty. The impact was profound: monasteries, parishes, and entire communities were divided as loyalties split between Rome and Avignon. The ensuing chaos lasted for decades, and it wasn't until the Council of Constance in 1417—a monumental gathering of European leaders, theologians, and reformers—that the schism could be resolved. Nevertheless, even the council's hard-won victory left scars that would take generations to heal, marking a turning point in the Church's long struggle to balance spiritual ideals with the harsh demands of political power.

Beyond their immediate personal failings and administrative shortcomings, the reigns of Boniface VIII and Urban VI reveal broader truths about the nature of leadership. Even the greatest institutions risk unraveling when power is wielded without a foundation in wisdom and compromise. Boniface's aspirations for unquestioned papal supremacy were demonstrably at odds with the emergent spirit of national sovereignty and the rise of modern statehood. His decrees, no matter how boldly stated, couldn't override the shifting allegiances and pragmatic realities of European politics. Meanwhile, Urban's descent into cruelty and paranoia laid bare the perils of internal discord. His heavy-handed measures did nothing to strengthen the Church; instead, they hastened its fragmentation and left it vulnerable to external manipulation. Their legacies are enduring warnings that unchecked ambition, ideological inflexibility, and personal vendettas can destabilize even those institutions claiming divine authority.

The aftermath of these turbulent papacies forced the Church into a painful process of introspection and adaptation. As the immediate fallout of Boniface's ideological conflicts and Urban's tumultuous governance became apparent, efforts to restore order and credibility began to take shape. The fraught relationship between spiritual leadership and secular power, once taken for granted, now demanded a reevaluation of long-held principles. Scholars, theologians, and political reformers—many of whom were inspired by the controversies that had splintered Christendom—began advocating for reforms that would redefine the papacy's role. These reform movements, building upon the spirit of earlier initiatives like the Gregorian Reforms, sought to erect safeguards against the excesses of personal ambition. Among these early reformers, consensus gradually emerged that spiritual authority must be underpinned by divine inspiration, pragmatic governance, and accountability.

Cultural reflections throughout Europe mirrored these seismic shifts in power dynamics. Chroniclers recorded their observations in illuminated manuscripts that detailed these papal reigns' grandeur and corruption. Poets and satirists cast Boniface and Urban as tragic figures—symbols of once-sacred offices that earthly aspirations had corrupted. In fiery sermons and biting pamphlets, preachers and common folk alike decried the moral decay of an institution that had once been the embodiment of divine will. Artistic works from the period, ranging from stained glass depictions to intricate frescoes, captured scenes of ecclesiastical triumph and ignominious downfall. Such cultural productions ensured that the era's lessons—of ambition unchecked and power misused—would be passed down through generations as a constant reminder of the delicate equilibrium between the sacred and the secular.

The debates ignited by the papacies of Boniface VIII and Urban VI extended far beyond immediate political or theological circles. Their reigns became central topics at heated gatherings in courtrooms, universities, and church councils alike, prompting discussions that questioned the legitimacy of papal claims and the very nature of divine governance. Disputes over the limits of the papal mandate, the kings' rights, and the councils' role in adjudicating such conflicts laid the groundwork for a new form of political thought. This intellectual ferment would eventually contribute to the evolution of modern statecraft and the idea that the rule of law must balance political authority. This foundational concept endures in contemporary democratic societies.

Moreover, the impact of these controversial papacies was felt in every corner of medieval Europe, influencing the policies and strategies of monarchs. The disillusionment stemming from the papacy's actions emboldened rulers to pursue greater independence, gradually eroding the centralized spiritual authority that the Church had once wielded without contest. This power shift was a prelude to the later emergence of nation-states, where secular governments began to define their authority separate from the ancient ecclesiastical hierarchy. The legacy of Boniface and Urban isn't confined strictly to the annals of Church history—it's interwoven with the broader evolution of Western political institutions.

In reflecting on these transformative chapters of medieval history, one must grapple with the enduring questions of governance and morality. How does one reconcile the pursuit of divine truth with the practical demands of political power? What mechanisms must be in place to ensure those entrusted with spiritual authority are held accountable to their faith and followers? The struggles, crises, and eventual reforms that followed the reigns of Boniface VIII and Urban VI offer enduring insights into these questions. Their stories reveal that leadership challenges are as timeless as they are universal; whether in medieval Christendom or modern politico-religious contexts, ambition must be tempered by prudence, and authority must always be balanced by accountability.

Ultimately, the turbulent legacies of Pope Boniface VIII and Pope Urban VI underscore a profound lesson: that the institutions we hold sacred, no matter how divinely inspired, remain intrinsically human. Their power, ambition, and equally human failings can elevate and undermine a society's collective spirit. Their actions, replete with bold declarations of supremacy and catastrophic missteps, forced the Church to confront its vulnerabilities and, ultimately, to evolve. In doing so, their reigns set in motion a series of events and reforms that would pave the way for a more measured, accountable exercise of authority—a transformation that, in many ways, continues to echo in the modern world.

Thus, as we consider the legacies of these turbulent papacies, we're reminded that the accurate measure of leadership lies not in the unyielding assertion of power but in the capacity to adapt, reform, and balance competing demands. The unforgettable clash between the doctrinal declarations of Boniface VIII and the chaotic reign of Urban VI inspires not only historical reflection but also a timeless call for wisdom in governance—a call that resonates as strongly today as it did in the troubled days of medieval Europe. Through this lens, the histories of Boniface and Urban aren't merely cautionary tales but rather profound lessons in the ongoing human quest to reconcile the divine with the earthly, and to forge institutions that rise above the limitations of their time.

Chapter Seven

The Borgia Legacy
Scandal and Splendor
in Renaissance Rome
(1492–1503)

In the twilight of the 15th century, a new era of dominance and decadence was born as Rome simmered with ambition, and the scent of incense mingled with the aroma of spiced wine. Pope Alexander VI—Rodrigo Borgia—rose like a phoenix amid political intrigue and fervent whispers. His ascent to the papacy in 1492 wasn't an ordained miracle but a masterstroke of human ambition, executed through calculated bribery and maneuvers that transformed him from a shrewd cardinal into the sovereign of a dynasty that would haunt history. Under his watchful eye, the spiritual symbol of Christendom became entangled with the terrestrial power plays of mortal men and women, setting a precedent for a papacy steeped in opulent sin and calculated corruption.

When Alexander VI was crowned, Rome became his chessboard: a labyrinth of secret corridors, sumptuous banquet halls, and shadowed cloisters where alliances were forged over hushed confidences and gold coins exchanged like blessings. Unabashedly, he elevated his illegitimate progeny, bending the rigid structures of Church propriety to his will. Cesare, once destined for an ecclesiastical life, cast aside sacred vestments to become the embodiment of martial ambition. Meanwhile, his daughter Lucrezia was immersed not in quiet devotions but in the labyrinthine intrigues of Europe's highest politics; her marriages were arranged like pieces on a board to secure favors and bind formidable allies to the Borgia cause.

Rome under Alexander VI wasn't merely a center of piety; it was an arena of carnal indulgence and relentless pursuit of pleasure where the divine collided with the decadence of earthly desires. One story whispered through centuries captures this collision in startling detail: the legendary Banquet of Chestnuts. On a crisp autumn evening in 1501, inside the cool, candlelit recesses of the Apostolic Palace, an atmosphere of both splendor and depravity permeated the air. Elaborate tapestries draped the walls as the flickering glow of myriad candles revealed sumptuous table settings laden with goblets of ruby wine and platters overloaded with exotic delicacies. Nevertheless, as opulence reigned, a more scandalous scene unfolded—a night during which fifty courtesans, draped in delicate silks that revealed and concealed in equal measure, performed their art for the assembled elite.

In this feverish reverie of the senses, servants scattered fresh chestnuts upon gleaming marble floors—a seemingly innocuous act that transformed into an absurd yet sensual contest. Moving with a grace that bent the laws of decorum, the courtesans were compelled to crawl on all fours, their lithe forms gliding over the cold stone as onlookers wagered in hushed tones on whose grace would best captivate the room. Laughter mingled with gasps of admiration and scandal as the night spiraled into an orgy of excess where prizes weren't measured in gold but in whispered promises of forbidden pleasure. Though some later chroniclers and critics dismissed these accounts as grotesque fabrications designed to tarnish the Borgia name, the enduring legends of that night speak to an era in which the boundaries of sanctity and sin were dangerously blurred.

Away from the indulgent debauchery of liturgical corridors and masquerade-like celebrations, Cesare Borgia strode forward as the instrument of his father's ambitions: a warrior whose very heartbeat resonated with the cold rhythm of conquest. For him, the art of war was a symphony orchestrated with ruthless precision. His campaigns, which swept through the provinces of Romagna and beyond, unfolded like dark ballets. Armies marched like ominous storms under his command, leaving behind a trail of shattered villages, ruined alliances, and broken spears. In a moment of macabre brilliance, Cesare once lured a band of mercenary captains to the unsuspecting calm of Senigallia, extending an olive branch of false peace. It was within those ancient walls that a massacre erupted—a tableau of betrayal so chilling that it echoed through subsequent generations as a brutal reminder that in the pursuit of power, trust was an illusion as fragile as spun glass.

The calculated ruthlessness of Cesare didn't go unnoticed. Observing his maneuvers from the margins of safe observation was Niccolò Machiavelli, who would later distill Cesare's unyielding realism into the seminal treatise, The Prince. For Machiavelli, Cesare was both muse and admonition—a living embodiment of power seized by those who dared to step beyond moral constraints and embrace a darker, more pragmatic truth. Indeed, Cesare's violent and unrepentant methods were a testament to a world in which honor was defined not by chivalric ideals but by the unforgiving logic of survival and dominance. Nevertheless, as is often the harsh decree of fate, the tempest that was Cesare eventually faltered. With the sudden and mysterious demise of Alexander VI in 1503, the protective aura of the Borgia papacy crumbled, leaving Cesare exposed to the vengeful ambitions of former allies-turned-foes. Betrayed and besieged, he was forced into exile—a tragic figure whose once-glorious conquest ended in obscurity far from the vibrant heart of Rome.

While Cesare embodied the fierce, warlike aspect of the Borgia legacy, Lucrezia Borgia emerged as a figure cloaked in the enigma of whispered legend and misunderstood virtue. History would often depict her as a calculating seductress or a hapless victim—rarely allowing space for a multifaceted reality. In truth, Lucrezia navigated an existence where every marriage was a carefully orchestrated chess move designed to advance her family's interests and secure their unyielding grip on the dangerous yet alluring tapestry of Italian politics. Her union with Giovanni Sforza unraveled amid scandal and bitter rumor, and her subsequent marriage to Alfonso of Aragon was mired in both political ambition and tragic misfortune. There were even darker murmurs—allegations of poisonings and nefarious plots that painted her as the dark mistress of lethal secrets.

Nevertheless, even as these stories assailed her reputation, Lucrezia's inner light shone unexpectedly. In the safer, more cultured enclaves of Ferrara, she embraced a role as a patron of the arts, fostering poets, scholars, and artists whose works would transcend the sordid legend of her family. Though history may have schemed to reduce her to a single stereotype—either a femme fatale or a sorrowful martyr—Lucrezia's true identity lay in the interplay between these extreme portrayals. She was, at once, an instrument of political strategy and a cultivated lady who sought beauty and wisdom in a world dominated by betrayal.

As the years passed and the echo of Alexander VI's presence faded with his sudden and painful collapse in 1503, Rome found itself at a crossroads. The infamous pope, whose days had been marked by unholy indulgence and the brazen elevation of personal ambition, left behind a legacy that was both a magnet and a curse. His death, shrouded in mystery and whispered theories of poisoning or divine retribution, ignited a cautious relief among some and a profound sense of uncertainty among others. For beneath the veneer of ecclesiastical reform and renewed piety, the seeds of dissent sown by his corrupt administration had taken root. The scandals of his reign had not only scandalized the faithful but had also contributed to a growing public outcry for a renewal of the Church. This clarion call would eventually help spark the flames of the Protestant Reformation.

The Council of Trent, convened in the mid-16th century to rectify the rampant abuses and moral decay that had, in part, taken shape during Alexander VI's tumultuous papacy, aimed to cleanse the Church of the very excesses that the Borgias had epitomized. However, even as the sacred halls of the Vatican rang with renewed vows of chastity and discipline, the legacy of the Borgias couldn't be easily expunged. Their story became a permanent scar on the annals of the Church—an eternal reminder that the interplay of power, greed, and ambition remains a potent force capable of corrupting even the most hallowed institutions.

In the end, the Borgia legacy endures not as a faded chapter in a dusty history book but as a vivid, living myth that continues to captivate the imagination and evoke both revulsion and admiration. Their lives, draped in opulence and marred by scandal, offer an unvarnished look at the human condition: a mixture of remarkable talent and unyielding vice, of moments of transcendent beauty and acts of unimaginable cruelty. Even as the marble halls and frescoed ceilings of modern Rome have been restored and renewed, the ghostly echoes of the Borgias still seem to linger in every shadowed corridor, every intimate whisper in a quiet chapel. They remind us that in the grand tapestry of human ambition, the line between sanctity and sin is often imperceptible, blurred by the equally potent forces of desire and despair.

Thus, the saga of Pope Alexander VI and his illustrious children remains an enduring parable of power—a lesson in the costs of excess and the eternal allure of notoriety. It's a story told not merely in the dry recounting of dates and deeds but in the passionate, vivid recollections of a Renaissance era that celebrated life in all its unvarnished complexity. As readers journey through the opulent courts and dangerous intrigue of that world, they're invited to ponder the timeless interplay of virtue and vice, the eternal dance between light and shadow—a dance that, long after the voices of the Borgias have faded, continues to echo through the corridors of history.

Chapter Eight

The Papacy and the New World: Authority, Exploration, and Exploitation.

As the Renaissance Popes were embroiled in their pursuit of temporal power and artistic grandeur within Europe, a new, unforeseen frontier opened across the oceans, presenting the papacy with both an unprecedented opportunity for global evangelization and a profound moral dilemma. As European mariners pushed the boundaries of the known world, a powerful concept emerged: the "Doctrine of Discovery," asserting the right of Christian nations to claim lands not already under Christian rule. This assertion frequently sought, and often received, papal endorsement, intertwining spiritual authority with secular ambition. This collision forged a complex and often tragic narrative where the "divine aspiration" to spread Christianity became deeply entangled with the "human ambition" for conquest and the brutal realities of "exploitation." The papacy, as the supreme spiritual authority of Christendom, found itself in the unique, powerful, and ultimately challenging position of mediating claims to newly "discovered" lands, even as the ethical implications of subjugation and violence unfolded. This chapter explores how popes navigated, shaped, and at times tragically failed to adequately address the profound "shadows" cast by European expansion from the late 15th to the mid-16th century, creating a lasting and uncomfortable legacy.

The theological and legal groundwork for papal involvement in overseas expansion was laid well before Columbus's momentous voyages. Portugal, a pioneering maritime power, had steadily been exploring down the coast of West Africa, seeking new trade routes and allies against Islamic powers. To legitimize their conquests and claim exclusive rights, they turned to Rome. Pope Nicholas V (1447–1455) answered their call with the seminal bull Romanus Pontifex in 1455. This document granted King Afonso V of Portugal the right to "invade, search out, capture, vanquish, and subdue all Saracens and pagans whatsoever, and other enemies of Christ wheresoever placed, and the kingdoms, duchies, principalities... and to reduce their persons to perpetual slavery." While rooted in the context of the Reconquista and the ongoing struggle against non-Christian powers, Romanus Pontifex provided a powerful theological and legal justification for European powers to assert dominion over non-Christian lands and their inhabitants. It implicitly linked Christian evangelization with territorial conquest and the outright enslavement of entire populations, setting an early, deeply controversial precedent that would cast a long "shadow" over the Church's global mission.

The ethical stakes for the papacy rose exponentially with Christopher Columbus's first voyage in 1492 and his return with news of vast new lands and peoples. The Spanish monarchs, Ferdinand and Isabella, eager to secure their claims against potential Portuguese rivalry, swiftly appealed to Rome for papal arbitration. Pope Alexander VI (1492–1503), whose pontificate was simultaneously marked by the worldly machinations and nepotism discussed in the previous chapter, seized this unprecedented moment to assert papal authority on a truly global scale. In 1493, he issued a series of five bulls, most notably Inter Caetera. This pivotal document drew an imaginary line of demarcation 100 leagues west of the Azores and Cape Verde islands, granting Spain exclusive rights to all lands west of that line, provided they were not already under Christian rule, with a corresponding grant to Portugal for lands to the east. Alexander VI's action was far more than a mere territorial division; it effectively bestowed papal legitimacy upon the Spanish and Portuguese crowns to evangelize the indigenous populations and establish sovereign control over them. While ostensibly framed as a means to spread Christianity, Inter Caetera profoundly contributed to the legal and moral framework that facilitated European conquest, colonization, and the systematic subjugation of vast indigenous populations, directly showcasing the "shadows" of papal involvement in geopolitical power plays.

As the conquest proceeded, the brutal realities of colonization—including forced labor (the encomienda system), cultural destruction, and the horrifying decimation of indigenous populations through disease, violence, and exploitation—began to provoke fierce moral and theological debate within the Church itself. Amidst the brutality, it's crucial to acknowledge the genuine, often courageous, spiritual devotion of many missionaries who sought to bring the Christian faith to new lands, driven by a sincere belief in salvation. Yet, even these sincere efforts were inextricably bound to the mechanisms of conquest. Voices of "courageous testimony" emerged, directly challenging the prevailing justifications for exploitation. Among the most prominent was the Dominican friar Bartolomé de las Casas. Having arrived in the New World as a settler, Las Casas became a fierce and tireless advocate for indigenous rights, dedicating his life to denouncing the atrocities committed by the conquistadors. His transformation from a beneficiary of the encomienda system to its most vocal opponent makes his testimony all the more compelling, illustrating the profound moral reckoning that conscience could demand even in the face of immense vested interests. His harrowing accounts of Spanish brutality and his passionate arguments for the inherent human dignity and rights of Native Americans reached the highest levels of the Spanish court and, crucially, Rome.

Las Casas's unwavering advocacy, along with the intellectual firepower of Spanish theologians at the School of Salamanca (particularly Francisco de Vitoria, who championed international law and the inherent rights of all peoples), compelled the papacy to re-evaluate its initial stance. This led to a pivotal moment under Pope Paul III (1534–1549). In 1537, Paul III issued the bull Sublimis Deus, a landmark declaration that stands as a profound attempt to assert the Church's moral authority against rampant abuse. In an age where the humanity of indigenous peoples was routinely questioned to justify their subjugation, Paul III's clear affirmation was a direct and unprecedented challenge to the prevailing colonial ideology, attempting to draw a firm moral line. The bull unequivocally stated that Native Americans were rational beings with souls, fully capable of receiving the Christian faith. Crucially, it condemned their enslavement and affirmed their right to liberty and property, declaring that "the Indians are truly men and that they are not only capable of understanding the Catholic Faith, but also, according to our information, they desire exceedingly to receive it." Sublimis Deus was a vital, if belated, attempt by the papacy to push back against the dehumanization that underpinned much of the exploitation and to assert a universal principle of human dignity.

Despite the profound ethical statements of popes like Paul III, the gap between papal decree and colonial practice remained vast. The economic and political imperatives of the burgeoning European empires, coupled with the immense distances and the decentralized nature of colonial administration, often overshadowed the moral exhortations from Rome. Sublimis Deus, while a powerful document, was met with resistance by some colonial authorities and its enforcement was frequently inconsistent. The debates initiated by Las Casas and the legal-theological arguments of the School of Salamanca continued for decades, profoundly influencing later Catholic thought on natural law and human rights, but they could not immediately halt the tide of exploitation. Thus, the initial papal authorizations, though later nuanced and challenged from within the Church, remained a potent symbol of the Church's historical entanglement with the dynamics of European expansion and its resulting "shadows."

The Papacy's engagement with the New World in this crucial early period (late 15th to mid-16th century) thus reveals a complex interplay of evangelistic zeal and geopolitical influence, leading to both profound "sanctity" in the genuine efforts of some missionaries and deep "shadows" of exploitation and moral compromise. The initial bulls laid a foundation for conquest and subjugation, while later interventions attempted to correct its gravest moral abuses. This era stands as a powerful testament to the Church's ongoing struggle to reconcile its divine mission with the unyielding realities of human ambition and the devastating consequences of unchecked power. The theological and legal precedents set during this era continued to influence colonial policies for centuries, and their legacy remains a subject of profound historical and moral reckoning even in the modern Church, demonstrating how papal authority, even with a stated spiritual aim, could be co-opted or insufficiently applied to legitimize actions that would echo as profound historical injustices for centuries to come.

Chapter Nine

Reformation & Resistance – Pope Leo X and Pope Clement VII (1513–1534)

Pope Leo X: Renaissance Pope and Reformation Catalyst

In the twilight of the 15th century, a new era of dominance and decadence was born as Rome simmered with ambition, and the scent of incense mingled with the aroma of spiced wine. Pope Leo X, born Giovanni di Lorenzo de' Medici, ascended to the papacy in 1513 when the Catholic Church was the center of cultural magnificence and the epicenter of financial and spiritual corruption. His reign, lasting until 1521, is a tapestry woven with the vibrant threads of Renaissance art, political maneuvering, and religious ideology, yet marred by a neglect of fiscal responsibility and moral accountability.

In Leo X's Rome, the sacred and the secular intermingled—a court renowned for its patronage of great artists, intellectuals, and philosophers was also one that indulged in lavish spending and embraced practices which, in time, would undermine the Church's dominion.

Drawing on the illustrious legacy of the Medici family, Leo X inherited considerable wealth and a passion for art, learning, and humanism that had defined Renaissance Florence. Determined to leave an indelible mark on history, he transformed the Vatican into a crucible of culture where masterpieces by Raphael and Michelangelo flourished. His support wasn't merely financial; it was ideological. Leo X believed the Church could and should serve as a bastion of refined taste and intellectual discourse. Under his watch, courtiers, scholars, and artists mingled in a heady mix of creation and debate, embodying the spirit of the Renaissance.

Nevertheless, even as the arts ascended, the financial practices underpinning Leo X's generosity sowed the seeds of a broader crisis. The exorbitant spending required to commission art, maintain a sprawling court, and fund ambitious architectural projects—most notably the rebuilding of St. Peter's Basilica—strained the Vatican's treasury. To support his grand vision, Leo X increasingly turned to the sale of indulgences. What began as a theological practice intended to offer remission from temporal punishment after forgiven sins slowly degenerated into a monetized lifeline for papal finances.

Enabled by the revolutionary power of Gutenberg's printing press, indulgences were mass-produced and disseminated with unprecedented speed. This new technology, once celebrated for its capacity to spread knowledge, now served as an instrument of financial exploitation. The Church issued certificates that promised absolution in exchange for monetary contributions—a commodification of salvation that quickly drew ire from the devout and the learned alike. The indulgence system became more than an administrative tool; it evolved into a potent symbol of corruption and the misuse of spiritual authority.

Central to the unfolding scandal was the figure of Johann Tetzel, a Dominican friar who emerged as the public face of indulgence sales. Born around 1465 in Pirna, Saxony, Tetzel rose through the ranks of the Dominican order to become an itinerant preacher whose persuasive oratory and theatrical style left a lasting impression on the German populace. Appointed by Archbishop Albert of Mainz—a high-ranking churchman heavily indebted due to the accrual of numerous benefices—Tetzel was charged with a singular, controversial task: to raise funds for the rebuilding of St. Peter's Basilica by selling indulgences.

Tetzel's approach was both charismatic and ruthless. With his impassioned sermons, he instilled in his listeners a profound fear of the torments of purgatory. His famous refrain, "As soon as the coin in the coffer rings, the soul from purgatory springs," echoed through towns and villages, creating an almost messianic association between wealth and salvation. Tetzel's sales pitches were elaborate, combining vivid imagery of divine retribution with the promise of immediate redemption. He addressed large audiences in makeshift basilicas and town squares, ensuring that every word resonated with those desperate for spiritual relief. For many, the purchase of an indulgence served not only as a form of penance but as a tangible safeguard for the eternal fate of their loved ones.

In his sermons, Tetzel left little room for nuance; he argued that the Church's treasury of merits—acquired from the good works of saints and the forgiveness of sins—could be drawn upon to alleviate the anguish of purgatory for both the living and the dead. This controversial doctrine implied that a simple monetary contribution could diminish or even erase the temporal punishment that awaited sinful souls. For affluent merchants, minor nobles, and even ordinary peasants, indulgences became a transactional assurance—a certificate of absolution that promised their families a shortcut to heaven. The commercialization of faith, however, came at a high moral and theological cost: many within the Church itself began to question whether salvation could truly be bought rather than earned through sincere repentance and devotion.

Though effective at raising funds, Tetzel's methods were widely denounced by theologians who criticized the notion that repentance could be so readily circumvented. As many scholars later noted, Tetzel's extreme assertions not only flouted traditional teachings but betrayed a dangerous departure from the Church's mandate to guide the faithful toward true spiritual renewal. His claims that indulgences could pardon sins yet to be committed and thoroughly secure the souls of the dead were seen by many, and later reformers, as a mockery of genuine penance and contrition.

The controversy surrounding Tetzel's campaign didn't remain confined to his sermons alone. His relentless promotion of indulgences provided the spark that ignited the broader conflagration of dissent within the Church. In the spring of 1517, as Tetzel preached his aggressive sales pitch in Jüterbog, near Wittenberg, he unwittingly set the stage for one of the most significant challenges to papal authority in history. Martin Luther, a German monk and theologian, had grown increasingly disillusioned with the Church's practices. Confronted with Tetzel's claims and the evident exploitation of the faithful, Luther took up a pen against the prevailing orthodoxy—resulting in the famously bold act of nailing his Ninety-five Theses to the doors of the Castle Church on October 31, 1517.

Luther's Theses weren't merely a list of grievances but a profound theological rebuke of the commercialization of repentance. By documenting his objections in clear, forceful language, Luther challenged the notion that salvation could be reduced to a financial transaction. His critique resonated with scholars, clergy, and laypeople alike, rapidly spreading throughout Germany via the printing press that had earlier fueled Tetzel's sales. The rapid dissemination of Luther's ideas on paper and in impassioned public debates forced the Church to reckon with a growing movement that questioned its spiritual legitimacy.

Even as the controversy intensified, Leo X appeared initially indifferent to the mounting criticism. Embarrassed perhaps by the wholesale commercialization of sacred practice, yet unwilling to relinquish the financial lifeline that indulgences provided, the Pope dismissed Luther's protests as the outbursts of an incorrigible friar. His administration continued to endorse the indulgence system even as public sentiment began to sway. It was only when the pressure became insurmountable that Leo X reluctantly sanctioned the excommunication of Luther in 1521. This irrevocable act, intended to silence dissent, instead proved to be a pivotal moment, precipitating the Protestant Reformation—a seismic shift that would forever alter the religious landscape of Europe.

Beyond his reign's theological and fiscal dimensions, Leo X's papacy was entrenched in the labyrinthine world of Renaissance politics. At a time when Europe was a chessboard of shifting alliances, the Papal States attempted to maneuver between the ambitions of France, Spain, and the Holy Roman Empire. Leo X's diplomatic endeavors were as extravagant as his court. His display of opulence at elaborate banquets and state ceremonies was intended to underscore the Church's transcendent authority, yet it simultaneously exposed the vanity and extravagance that plagued his administration. Portraits, like Raphael's celebrated rendering of Leo X with Cardinals Giulio de' Medici and Luigi de' Rossi, capture not only the physical corpulence of the Pope but also the excess that defined his rule. These works of art, resplendent in detail and imbued with symbolism, serve as enduring reminders of a leadership deeply conflicted by splendor and failings.

The pervasive culture of indulgence was mirrored in every corner of the Vatican. Not only did the sale of indulgences corrupt the sanctity of spiritual practice, but it also gave rise to a broader environment of moral decay. The clergy, often complicit in misappropriating funds, embarked on a lifestyle marked by luxury and self-interest. Nepotism and favoritism ensured power remained within a tightly knit circle of relatives and loyalists, most notably within the Medici clan. Scholarly debates soon emerged regarding the actual cost of such practices—not merely in the depletion of the Vatican's coffers but in the erosion of an institution's moral authority.

As Leo X's health waned and his reign neared its inevitable conclusion, the legacy of his papacy began to crystallize into a cautionary tale. His death in 1521—whether due to poisoning, pneumonia, or the accumulated toll of an overindulgent lifestyle—symbolized the collapse of a system unable to evolve amidst a rapidly changing world. The religious and financial imbalances he had nurtured had sown the seeds of transformation; the fragmented unity of Christendom now splintered along the new lines drawn by Protestant reformers and secular powers alike.

In retrospect, Leo X's tenure stands as a study in contradictions. Here was a pope who celebrated the heights of artistic expression and human intellect yet whose insatiable pursuit of wealth and prestige undermined the spiritual and moral foundations of the Church. His lavish patronage ushered in what many consider the zenith of Renaissance art and culture. However, precisely this opulence—and the consequent financial improprieties—opened the door to reform movements that challenged centuries of ecclesiastical tradition.

At the heart of this confluence of art, politics, and commerce was the deeply transformative—and ultimately tragic—phenomenon of indulgences. It's impossible to separate the theological innovations of the period from the commercial interests that exploited them. The narrative of Leo X cannot be told without recognizing the profound impact of Johann Tetzel's flamboyant salesmanship. Tetzel's life, with its dramatic rise and swift fall from grace, encapsulates the hubris of an era that placed monetary gain above spiritual integrity. While designed to secure funding for sacred projects, his methods inadvertently exposed contradictions inherent in a system where redemption was auctioned to the highest bidder.

Pope Clement VII and the Sack of Rome

In the explosive aftermath of Leo X's scandal-riddled reign, Clement VII stepped into the papal seat in 1523 like a reluctant hero cast into the eye of a violent storm. His pontificate was no serene chapter of ecclesiastical diplomacy—it was an era steeped in raw chaos, relentless political intrigue, and dramatic upheaval. Almost immediately, the brutal reality of his new position became apparent: his ascension coincided with the flowering of deep societal fissures and a crumbling spiritual façade that once cloaked the Church in an air of divine invincibility.

At the heart of his troubled tenure lay the cataclysmic Sack of Rome in 1527—a moment that transformed history into a living nightmare. In a scene reminiscent of a fevered dream, mercenary legions, their ambition untethered and loyalties fleeting, descended upon the Eternal City with a ferocity that defied belief. The invaders unleashed their violence upon Rome with the efficiency of a well-oiled machine, stripping the sacred of its sanctity. In that grim, heart-wrenching moment, ancient relics were desecrated, cherished treasures plundered, and the symbols of Christendom were scattered like broken pieces of an irreparable mosaic. It wasn't merely a military disaster but an existential crisis that shattered the myth of an unassailable divine shield around the papacy.

For Clement, the devastation was a multifaceted trial. Beyond the immediate horror of the Sack, it unraveled the intricate tapestry of international alliances in which the Church had long been enmeshed. The Italian peninsula, a patchwork of rival city-states and quarreling principalities, was a veritable labyrinth of betrayals, where shifting allegiances and political expediencies eclipsed spiritual concerns at every turn. Each decision and every diplomatic foray Clement attempted was thwarted by a reality where temporal power reigned supreme, casting a long shadow over any flicker of moral authority. A volatile political landscape continually undermined his efforts to stem the tide of chaos. In this landscape, the ideals of faith were both weaponized and manipulated for worldly gain.

At the same time, these events' seismic impact reverberated far beyond Rome's confines. Across Europe, the wash of disillusionment set off a cultural renaissance of dissent. The excesses of Leo X's indulgence system, barely contained in the gilded halls of the Vatican, collided with the carnage of the Sack, giving voice to an emerging public outcry. In bustling city squares, artists and poets risked everything to pen biting satires, crafting pamphlets and plays that skewered the opulence and moral decay of the papal court. What was once the unquestioned divine authority of the Church now became the subject of cantankerous debates and irreverent mockery. This narrative elevated public discourse and planted the seeds of modern critique.

Economic and technological forces further accelerated this transformative period. The rapid spread of the printing press was akin to a revolution in mass communication that transformed hushed murmurs of reform into a resounding clamor for change. Ideas that challenged the longstanding practices of indulgence and accepted doctrine exploded onto the stage, broadcast to an ever-growing literate public. This democratization of knowledge exposed the Church's manipulative financial practices and laid bare the conflation of sacred duty with monetary greed. Merchants, scholars, and ordinary citizens alike began questioning the ethics of a system that diverted spiritual incomes into ostentatious displays of wealth and power. This convergence of commerce, technology, and theology fundamentally redrew the map of religious and political authority, setting in motion a process that would eventually contribute to the emergence of modern nation-states.

Amid the chaos, intense theological debates roared to life. The reverberations of scandal and bloodshed forced scholars and theologians to reexamine age-old doctrines. Questions about sin, redemption, and the very nature of divine grace were no longer content to reside within the confines of ancient texts—they were thrust into the public arena and debated vigorously in courts, chapels, and town squares. As reformers questioned the commodification of salvation, new ideas challenged the Church's timeless tenets, heralding an irreversible shift in spiritual consciousness that echoed far into the future. The intellectual ferment of the early sixteenth century, alongside mounting moral outrage, transformed how religious authority was understood—even as the Church struggled to maintain its crumbling foundations.

Amid this maelstrom, Pope Clement VII navigated a treacherous landscape where each victory was hard-won and every setback a dramatic fall from grace. His papacy, marked by persistent attempts to restore order and reclaim divine legitimacy, symbolized resilience against overwhelming odds. Nevertheless, his struggles underscored a broader truth: that the era's spiritual, cultural, and political revolutions were inexorably intertwined. The upheavals during his reign didn't simply signal the decline of an old order; they also laid the groundwork for the transformative movements that would shape Europe for centuries to come. Clement's story is a testament to a period when the forces of history moved with an almost poetic ferocity, intertwining ambition, betrayal, and a ceaseless quest for renewal.

His journey amidst the ruins of a compromised papacy has left an indelible, vivid reminder of the tumult and splendor inherent in a world on the brink of modernity.

Legacy of Reform

The seeds of renewal were sown in the long shadow of the tumultuous reigns of Leo X and Clement VII. The widespread disillusionment and internal crisis prompted the Catholic Church to embark on a complicated reform process that would eventually culminate in the Counter-Reformation. The Council of Trent, convened between 1545 and 1563 amidst the simmering tensions of religious conflict, emerged as the Church's determined effort to address systemic abuse, reinforce doctrinal integrity, and reclaim its spiritual authority. The painful lessons from the indulgence crisis, the political debacles, and the moral decay of papal extravagance laid the enduring foundation for a transformative redefinition of ecclesiastical life.

Even as the controversies of this era reshaped the Church, they also left an indelible mark on the broader tapestry of Western history. The legacies of Leo X and Clement VII continue to echo in every brushstroke of Renaissance art and every printed word challenging ecclesiastical corruption. The robust debates on theology and governance and the myriad artistic expressions of popular dissent set a precedent for future generations. They underscore a timeless truth:

that even the most venerable institutions must adapt to evolving social, economic, and intellectual demands or risk irrelevance. In the interplay between resplendent patronage and moral responsibility, the excesses of papal extravagance became the catalyst for radical reform—a rebirth born out of a profound crisis that forever altered the course of Christianity and the political order of Europe.

Ultimately, the story of the early sixteenth century isn't solely of decline but also of renewal. It's a narrative that encompasses the dazzling achievements of Renaissance art, the transformative power of technological innovation, and the relentless human spirit's quest for authenticity and reform. Through struggle and dissent, the Church of this era was reformed, its long-held dogmas rigorously questioned, and its role in society fundamentally redefined. The echoes of that tumultuous period can still be heard today, reminding us that in the relentless march of history, even the mightiest institutions must evolve to remain true to their sacred purpose. The turbulent legacies of Leo X and Clement VII stand as enduring testaments to the possibility of redemption—a powerful reminder that a renewed commitment to faith, integrity, and moral leadership can arise from the crucible of controversy and crisis.

Chapter Ten

Harsh Decrees the Repressive Policies of Pope Paul IV (1555-1559)

The mid-sixteenth century was a crucible of counter-revolution—a time when rising religious zeal and the shifting winds of reform challenged the old order and demanded the Church's bold reassertion of authority. After the Protestant Reformation's early tremors, the Catholic establishment was determined to reclaim its long-guarded moral and institutional authority. In this charged atmosphere, saturated with anxiety over heresy and the rapid dissemination of radical ideas enabled by the new printing press, Pope Paul IV emerged as one of the period's most uncompromising defenders of traditional doctrine. His papacy, lasting from 1555 to 1559, heralded a regime dominated by severe reforms and ruthless decrees—policies designed to stamp out all dissent and reforge the Church in an image of absolute orthodoxy.

From his election, Paul IV exhibited an iron resolve to restore what he considered the true essence of Catholicism. Unlike some of his more lenient predecessors, his policies weren't marked by gradual reform or diplomatic compromise; instead, Paul IV's vision was purification by force. Central to his strategy was the establishment and vigorous expansion of the Roman Inquisition, an institutional mechanism proving one of the darkest legacies of his papacy. The Inquisition, restructured under his directive, was charged with not only identifying heretical ideas but also eradicating them through stringent tribunals and punitive measures. Papal bulls and official decrees from his reign leave little doubt: Paul IV saw himself as a divine sentinel, tasked with eradicating anything that threatened the sanctity of the faith—even if it meant subjecting his subjects to extreme punishment.

The legal framework he promulgated was ruthless. Harsh penalties were meted out to anyone suspected of deviating from the accepted doctrine. Trials were swift and often shrouded in secrecy, with confessions—frequently extracted under severe duress—serving as the primary instrument justifying extreme sentences. The atmosphere of terror fostered by these measures was palpable in marketplaces and the hushed corridors of monasteries alike. In many cities throughout

Italy and beyond, whispers circulated of individuals being forced to recant their beliefs under threats of torture or death. This climate of fear was compounded by the fact that Paul IV's decrees weren't confined solely to doctrinal infractions but extended to any display of intellectual dissent. The faithful, who once found solace in the Church as a bastion of spiritual security, increasingly lived under the shadow of state-sanctioned surveillance and persecution.

Economic factors played a significant role in this repressive policy regime. As the Church's wealth had long been intertwined with its power, Paul IV was determined to harness that resource to fund his crusade against heresy. Revenues were diverted to support the operations of the Inquisition, and new taxes were levied to underwrite the costs of building and maintaining prisons and tribunals. Detailed fiscal records from his papacy reveal that the Church's vast estates and monetary holdings were marshaled in service of what he deemed an essential mission: the defense of orthodoxy at all costs. This aggressive fiscal maneuvering had far-reaching implications; it drained resources that might have been devoted to charitable works and artistic patronage, further cementing the perception that the Church prioritized consolidating its temporal power over fulfilling its spiritual mission.

Technological advances such as the printing press fundamentally altered the dynamics of religious debate during this period. Paul IV's papacy was when the rapid dissemination of ideas—orthodox and heretical—could no longer be contained. Pamphlets denouncing his brutal methods circulated swiftly across the continent, reaching audiences far beyond the scholarly elite. The new media landscape allowed for an unprecedented level of public discourse; propaganda supporting his decrees was broadcast on one hand while equally fervent criticisms emerged simultaneously. This dual-edged use of print technology meant that while his policies were intended to crush dissent, they also inadvertently amplified opposition to the Church's brutality.

One of the most contentious aspects of Paul IV's rule was his treatment of groups deemed outside the acceptable bounds of the faith—primarily Jews and other non-Catholic communities. Under his decrees, measures were introduced that curtailed the rights of these populations, effectively isolating them from broader society. Laws were enacted that restricted Jewish settlement, imposed onerous taxes, and curtailed opportunities for non-Catholics to engage in public office or commercial enterprise. In many cities, entire quarters were marked by enforced segregation and discrimination—a policy justified as necessary for preserving the "purity" of Christendom, yet unequivocally seen by many contemporaries as a state-sanctioned form of institutional bigotry. These decrees not only marginalized and targeted communities but also deepened societal divisions and fostered an enduring legacy of alienation and resentment.

The cultural ramifications of these repressive policies were far-reaching. Art and literature of the period bear witness to the climate of fear and tension that characterized Paul IV's papacy. Artists, compelled by censorship and a desire to reflect on the human condition, produced works imbued with allegory and veiled critique. Satirical engravings and clandestine liturgical plays emerged from underground circles, using humor and symbolism to question the cruelty of the Inquisition and the severity of his decrees. Such works, though sometimes suppressed, circulated widely—appearing in private collections and illuminated manuscripts that depicted not just the power of the Church but also its moral contradictions. These cultural artifacts, emblematic of a society caught between orthodoxy and heresy, contributed to a broader counter-narrative that ultimately spurred later reform movements.

The political ramifications of Paul IV's decrees were equally profound. His uncompromising policies destabilized the long-established balance between Church and state that had characterized medieval politics for centuries. Rival factions within the Italian states and across Europe seized upon the oppressive nature of his reign to justify a reassertion of local and secular authority. In many instances, local rulers began to distance themselves from the centralized power of Rome, organizing their own judicial systems and local councils to resist ecclesiastical overreach. This shift wasn't merely a reaction against doctrinal rigidity but also a strategic move by emerging nation-states, which saw in the papal repression an opportunity to assert political independence. The fragmentation of political alliances that ensued contributed to the gradual process of decentralization, setting the stage for modern state governance.

Adding further depth to this multifaceted picture are personal narratives and eyewitness accounts that offer a humanizing glimpse into the suffering wrought by these policies. Letters from embattled clerics—scrawled in desperate tones on parchment, later preserved in monastic archives—reveal the anguish of witnessing a sacred institution turn its instruments of power against its people. One such account describes the humiliation of a local priest who was forced to witness his parishioners' public recantations in the town square and wrote of the "devastation of faith" that spread like wildfire through his community. Other testimonies, compiled in the margins of theological treatises, speak of families torn apart by relentless inquisitorial purges and neighbors compelled to betray longstanding bonds for fear of persecution. These poignant stories, preserved for posterity, underscore the heavy toll that the enforcement of orthodoxy could exact on individual lives and communal cohesion.

In a striking paradox, however, the very forcefulness of Paul IV's repression also helped galvanize a countercurrent of intellectual and spiritual resistance. As scholars, theologians, and ordinary citizens began questioning the righteousness of such uncompromising measures, a quiet yet persistent call for reform began to take root. Intellectual debates erupted in university halls and were carried forth by circulating treatises that critiqued the harshness of doctrinal enforcement. Figures such as emerging humanists argued that true orthodoxy must be tempered with mercy and that the spirit of Christianity was irreconcilable with the cruelty of the Inquisition. This burgeoning skepticism would, over time, form the seedbed for later reform movements—a process that eventually gave rise to the sweeping changes of the Counter-Reformation, inaugurated most notably by the Council of Trent.

The legacy of Pope Paul IV's papacy is thus a complex tapestry, interwoven with threads of doctrinal rigor, political ambition, cultural constraint, and the unyielding pursuit of reform. His drive for purity, however unyielding, was counterbalanced by the widespread repercussions of his policies. This legacy manifested in a profound division between the Church's lofty ideals and its terrestrial exercise of power. In the wake of his reign, critics and reformers alike were compelled to grapple with a sobering truth: that actual authority demands the steadfast defense of core principles and an enduring commitment to mercy, justice, and the open exchange of ideas.

Modern historians, revisiting the archival records, personal letters, satirical engravings, and legal documents from this turbulent period, debate the efficacy and morality of Paul IV's decrees. Some argue that his uncompromising stance was a necessary bulwark against the spread of heresy; others contend that the intolerant measures he employed only deepened social fractures and stifled progress. This ongoing dialogue is a testament to the enduring relevance of his reign—a reminder that the proper exercise of power must constantly walk the fine line between the defense of tradition and the imperative for human dignity.

Reflecting on this turbulent chapter of Church history, one is left with a complex but instructive portrait of an institution struggling to reconcile religious zeal with pragmatic governance. The harsh decrees of Pope Paul IV, while intended to fortify the Church against internal and external threats, inadvertently sowed the seeds of alienation and dissent that would later spur comprehensive reforms. His legacy—etched in stern edicts, ignominious trials, and the whispered laments of a beleaguered populace—remains a powerful lesson for all who wield authority. It underscores a fundamental truth: Pursuing doctrinal purity, when executed without compassion and accountability, can undermine the very foundations of moral leadership.

Thus, the story of Paul IV's papacy, with all its repressive measures, economic machinations, cultural ramifications, and enduring social impact, stands as a grand and cautionary chronicle. It compels us to consider the delicate balance required between tradition and progress. This balance must be maintained to preserve an institution's sanctity and ensure that the ideals of justice, mercy, and open dialogue prevail in the face of unyielding power. In this tapestry of harsh decrees and passionate dissent, we find the timeless struggle that continues to define the nature of authority and the persistent human quest for a more just and humane order.

Chapter Eleven

The Reformation's Crucible: Response and Rigidity (c. 1540s –1570s)

The seismic shockwaves of the Protestant Reformation, having already splintered Christendom and challenged the very foundations of papal authority, demanded a profound and systematic response from the Catholic Church. The spiritual landscape of Europe was fractured, doctrines were hotly contested, and the moral authority of the papacy was under unprecedented siege. As European mariners pushed the boundaries of the known world, a powerful concept emerged: the "Doctrine of Discovery," asserting the right of Christian nations to claim lands not already under Christian rule. This assertion frequently sought, and often received, papal endorsement, intertwining spiritual authority with secular ambition. Moving beyond initial, often inadequate, reactions and individual condemnations, the Church faced an existential crisis that necessitated deep internal reform and a clear reassertion of its identity and doctrine. This period, often termed the Catholic Reformation or Counter-Reformation, was not merely a reaction; it was a crucible in which the Church was forged anew, emerging with clearer theological boundaries, stricter discipline, and a renewed spiritual vigor. This chapter will delve into the critical contributions of Popes Paul III, Pius IV, and Pius V, who, from the mid-16th century to the early 1570s, guided the Church through its most challenging and transformative years, defining its assertive "response" to heresy and its unwavering institutional "rigidity" in defense of tradition.

The critical turning point towards a systematic response came with Pope Paul III (pontificate 1534-1549). Ascending the papal throne amidst escalating religious fragmentation and the palpable threat of further schism, Paul III, despite his own human failings and familial ambitions (common during the Renaissance Papacy), possessed the foresight and courage to recognize the urgent need for a General Council. This was a momentous decision, as the call for a council had been consistently resisted or delayed by his predecessors for decades, largely due to lingering fears of conciliarism—the idea that councils held authority superior to the pope. Despite immense political obstacles, including fierce rivalries between the Holy Roman Emperor Charles V and the French King Francis I, and widespread skepticism among cardinals and secular rulers alike, Paul III demonstrated the iron will and diplomatic acumen necessary to finally convene the long-awaited Council of Trent. Opening in December 1545 in the Alpine city of Trent, the Council's initial sessions, guided by Paul III's vision, immediately tackled fundamental Protestant challenges head-on. It firmly reaffirmed the authority of Sacred Tradition alongside Scripture as sources of divine revelation, a direct refutation of sola scriptura. Crucially, it addressed the contentious doctrine of justification, condemning the Protestant concept of "faith alone" (sola fide) and emphasizing the necessity of good works and the sacraments for salvation. During his pontificate, Paul III also took steps to strengthen the Roman Inquisition, an ancient tribunal revitalized to serve as a central instrument for defending doctrinal orthodoxy and combating heresy. Under Paul III's leadership, the Church also formally approved the Society of Jesus (Jesuits) in 1540, a dynamic new order that would become the papacy's intellectual and missionary vanguard in the Counter-Reformation, dedicated to education, evangelization, and unwavering obedience to the Pope. Paul III's determination to initiate Trent and approve the Jesuits was a courageous acknowledgment of the Church's internal problems and a decisive move towards a systematic Catholic renewal.

The Council of Trent, however, was not a swift affair. Plagued by political rivalries that led to boycotts by some rulers, outbreaks of plague that forced relocations, and shifting papal priorities, it experienced several suspensions and reconvenings over nearly two decades. These prolonged interruptions highlighted the immense difficulty of forging unity amidst deep theological divisions and undertaking such radical reform across a vast, fractured Christendom. It ultimately fell to Pope Pius IV (pontificate 1559-1565) to finally bring the monumental undertaking to its definitive conclusion. After years of suspension and intense diplomatic maneuvering, Pius IV successfully reconvened the Council for its crucial third and final sessions in 1562. With remarkable skill and a steady hand, he skillfully navigated the remaining contentious issues, particularly concerning the reforms of the episcopacy and the clergy, which had been sources of significant corruption and absenteeism. Under his guidance, the Council issued groundbreaking disciplinary decrees emphasizing episcopal residence (mandating bishops live in their dioceses), curbing the abuse of multiple benefices (holding several ecclesiastical offices), and, most significantly, mandating the establishment of seminaries for the proper education and moral formation of priests. These reforms were vital to addressing the widespread clerical ignorance and laxity that had fueled much of the initial discontent. The vision was to replace poorly educated and undisciplined clergy with well-trained, devout priests who could effectively minister to their flocks. In 1564, Pius IV formally promulgated all of Trent's decrees with the bull Benedictus Deus, ensuring their universal application throughout the Catholic world and establishing the Profession of Faith of Trent, which all bishops and priests were required to swear as a mark of strict adherence to orthodoxy. His achievement in successfully concluding the Council was monumental, providing the Church with an unambiguous doctrinal framework and a comprehensive blueprint for internal reform.

The true test of the Council's impact, however, lay in its rigorous implementation, a task embraced with unyielding determination by Pope Pius V (pontificate 1566-1572). A Dominican friar known for his personal asceticism, profound piety, and unwavering devotion to orthodoxy (he had previously served as a rigorous Grand Inquisitor), Pius V set about transforming the Church from the top down. He was instrumental in turning Trent's directives into practical realities, establishing commissions to oversee their enforcement and holding provincial councils to ensure local implementation. He published the Roman Catechism (1566) to provide clear, uniform instruction in Catholic doctrine for clergy and laity alike, becoming a standard text for generations. Most famously, he revised and published the Roman Breviary (1568) and the Roman Missal (1570). This standardization of the Divine Office and the Mass, often known as the "Tridentine Mass," unified Catholic worship across the globe for centuries to come, eliminating local variations and representing a significant act of both doctrinal clarity and centralized authority in stark contrast to the liturgical experimentation and fragmentation emerging in Protestant lands. This meant that Catholics from Rome to newly colonized territories would experience the same Mass, fostering a universal sense of identity and reverence. Pius V rigorously enforced episcopal residence, combated simony, and elevated morally upright figures to positions of power, setting a powerful personal example of piety and discipline that inspired many. His actions were not just about institutional reform; they fostered a profound spiritual renewal that directly impacted the daily lives of the faithful. With well-trained priests emerging from seminaries and a standardized, reverent liturgy, the quality of parish life improved significantly, emphasizing frequent confession, regular reception of communion, and renewed devotions such as the Rosary and the veneration of the saints. This era saw piety become more accessible and systematically guided, embodying the "sanctity" and spiritual renewal that the Council had called for. His pontificate also saw the continued use and enforcement of the Index of Forbidden Books, a powerful tool for controlling intellectual discourse and preventing the spread of what the Church deemed heretical or dangerous ideas, underscoring the "rigidity" aspect of the Counter-Reformation's defense of orthodoxy.

The combined efforts of these three popes, culminating in the Council of Trent and its immediate, zealous implementation, reshaped the Catholic Church fundamentally. Doctrinally, the Council presented a clear, authoritative, and uncompromising response to Protestant theology, leaving no ambiguity about Catholic teachings on grace, sacraments, the papacy, tradition, and the veneration of saints. This clarity also spurred a renaissance in systematic theology, with scholars producing comprehensive works that elucidated Catholic doctrine with new precision and rigor, often in direct dialogue with Protestant critiques. Institutionally, it mandated vital reforms that revitalized the clergy through seminary education and ensured proper pastoral care, while strengthening the Church's administrative structure and making it more efficient and centralized under renewed papal authority. The papacy itself emerged from Trent with its significantly enhanced authority, having successfully guided the Council and then overseen the universal implementation of its decrees, establishing a more direct and centralized control over the universal Church. This period also witnessed a flourishing of Catholic spirituality, with figures like St. Teresa of Ávila and St. John of the Cross leading a profound mystical revival that demonstrated the enduring vibrancy of Catholic spiritual life, rooted in intense prayer and profound theological understanding, providing a powerful "response" to the Reformation's challenges by emphasizing inward spiritual experience. Furthermore, the Counter-Reformation found powerful artistic expression in the emergent Baroque style, a vibrant and emotionally charged art form designed to inspire awe, devotion, and a renewed sense of Catholic triumph, contrasting sharply with Protestant iconoclasm and serving as a visual testament to the Church's renewed confidence. The Church that emerged from this crucible was a more disciplined, unified, and doctrinally coherent entity, ready to defend its faith and expand its reach with renewed purpose, including an invigorated drive for global missions, directly extending the work begun in the New World. This intense period of papal leadership marked a profound historical juncture where the Catholic Church, in confronting existential challenge, forged a resilient identity defined by both robust doctrinal "rigidity" and profound institutional and spiritual "response."

Chapter Twelve

Pope Clement VIII and the burning of Giordano Bruno at the stake (1600)

T he mid-sixteenth century was a crucible of counter-revolution—a time when rising religious zeal and the shifting winds of reform challenged the old order and demanded the Church's bold reassertion of authority. After the Protestant Reformation's early tremors, the Catholic establishment was determined to reclaim its long-guarded moral and institutional authority. In this charged atmosphere, saturated with anxiety over heresy and the rapid dissemination of radical ideas enabled by the new printing press, Pope Paul IV emerged as one of the period's most uncompromising defenders of traditional doctrine. His papacy, lasting from 1555 to 1559, heralded a regime dominated by severe reforms and ruthless decrees—policies designed to stamp out all dissent and reforge the Church in an image of absolute orthodoxy.

From his election, Paul IV exhibited an iron resolve to restore what he considered the true essence of Catholicism. Unlike some of his more lenient predecessors, his policies weren't marked by gradual reform or diplomatic compromise; instead, Paul IV's vision was purification by force. Central to his strategy was the establishment and vigorous expansion of the Roman Inquisition, an institutional mechanism proving one of the darkest legacies of his papacy. The Inquisition, restructured under his directive, was charged with not only identifying heretical ideas but also eradicating them through stringent tribunals and punitive measures. Papal bulls and official decrees from his reign leave little doubt: Paul IV saw himself as a divine sentinel, tasked with eradicating anything that threatened the sanctity of the faith—even if it meant subjecting his subjects to extreme punishment.

The legal framework he promulgated was ruthless. Harsh penalties were meted out to anyone suspected of deviating from the accepted doctrine. Trials were swift and often shrouded in secrecy, with confessions—frequently extracted under severe duress—serving as the primary instrument justifying extreme sentences. The atmosphere of terror fostered by these measures was palpable in marketplaces and the hushed corridors of monasteries alike. In many cities throughout Italy and beyond, whispers circulated of individuals being forced to recant their beliefs under threats of torture or death. This climate of fear was compounded by the fact that Paul IV's decrees weren't confined solely to doctrinal infractions but extended to any display of intellectual dissent. The faithful, who once found solace in the Church as a bastion of spiritual security, increasingly lived under the shadow of state-sanctioned surveillance and persecution.

Economic factors played a significant role in this repressive policy regime. As the Church's wealth had long been intertwined with its power, Paul IV was determined to harness that resource to fund his crusade against heresy. Revenues were diverted to support the operations of the Inquisition, and new taxes were levied to underwrite the costs of building and maintaining prisons and tribunals. Detailed fiscal records from his papacy reveal that the Church's vast estates and monetary holdings were marshaled in service of what he deemed an essential mission: the defense of orthodoxy at all costs. This aggressive fiscal maneuvering had far-reaching implications; it drained resources that might have been devoted to charitable works and artistic patronage, further cementing the perception that the Church prioritized consolidating its temporal power over fulfilling its spiritual mission.

Technological advances such as the printing press fundamentally altered the dynamics of religious debate during this period. Paul IV's papacy was when the rapid dissemination of ideas—orthodox and heretical—could no longer be contained. Pamphlets denouncing his brutal methods circulated swiftly across the continent, reaching audiences far beyond the scholarly elite. The new media landscape allowed for an unprecedented level of public discourse; propaganda supporting his decrees was broadcast on one hand while equally fervent criticisms emerged simultaneously. This dual-edged use of print technology meant that while his policies were intended to crush dissent, they also inadvertently amplified opposition to the Church's brutality.

One of the most contentious aspects of Paul IV's rule was his treatment of groups deemed outside the acceptable bounds of the faith—primarily Jews and other non-Catholic communities. Under his decrees, measures were introduced that curtailed the rights of these populations, effectively isolating them from broader society. Laws were enacted that restricted Jewish settlement, imposed onerous taxes, and curtailed opportunities for non-Catholics to engage in public office or commercial enterprise. In many cities, entire quarters were marked by enforced segregation and discrimination—a policy justified as necessary for preserving the "purity" of Christendom, yet unequivocally seen by many contemporaries as a state-sanctioned form of institutional bigotry. These decrees not only marginalized and targeted communities but also deepened societal divisions and fostered an enduring legacy of alienation and resentment.

The cultural ramifications of these repressive policies were far-reaching. Art and literature of the period bear witness to the climate of fear and tension that characterized Paul IV's papacy. Artists, compelled by censorship and a desire to reflect on the human condition, produced works imbued with allegory and veiled critique. Satirical engravings and clandestine liturgical plays emerged from underground circles, using humor and symbolism to question the cruelty of the Inquisition and the severity of his decrees. Such works, though sometimes suppressed, circulated widely—appearing in private collections and illuminated manuscripts that depicted not just the power of the Church but also its moral contradictions. These cultural artifacts, emblematic of a society caught between orthodoxy and heresy, contributed to a broader counter-narrative that ultimately spurred later reform movements.

The political ramifications of Paul IV's decrees were equally profound. His uncompromising policies destabilized the long-established balance between Church and state that had characterized medieval politics for centuries. Rival factions within the Italian states and across Europe seized upon the oppressive nature of his reign to justify a reassertion of local and secular authority. In many instances, local rulers began to distance themselves from the centralized power of Rome, organizing their own judicial systems and local councils to resist ecclesiastical overreach. This shift wasn't merely a reaction against doctrinal rigidity but also a strategic move by emerging nation-states, which saw in the papal repression an opportunity to assert political independence. The fragmentation of political alliances that ensued contributed to the gradual process of decentralization, setting the stage for modern state governance.

Adding further depth to this multifaceted picture are personal narratives and eyewitness accounts that offer a humanizing glimpse into the suffering wrought by these policies. Letters from embattled clerics—scrawled in desperate tones on parchment, later preserved in monastic archives—reveal the anguish of witnessing a sacred institution turn its instruments of power against its people. One such account describes the humiliation of a local priest who was forced to witness his parishioners' public recantations in the town square and wrote of the "devastation of faith" that spread like wildfire through his community. Other testimonies, compiled in the margins of theological treatises, speak of families torn apart by relentless inquisitorial purges and neighbors compelled to betray longstanding bonds for fear of persecution. These poignant stories, preserved for posterity, underscore the heavy toll that the enforcement of orthodoxy could exact on individual lives and communal cohesion.

In a striking paradox, however, the very forcefulness of Paul IV's repression also helped galvanize a countercurrent of intellectual and spiritual resistance. As scholars, theologians, and ordinary citizens began questioning the righteousness of such uncompromising measures, a quiet yet persistent call for reform began to take root. Intellectual debates erupted in university halls and were carried forth by circulating treatises that critiqued the harshness of doctrinal enforcement. Figures such as emerging humanists argued that true orthodoxy must be tempered with mercy and that the spirit of Christianity was irreconcilable with the cruelty of the Inquisition. This burgeoning skepticism would, over time, form the seedbed for later reform movements—a process that eventually gave rise to the sweeping changes of the Counter-Reformation, inaugurated most notably by the Council of Trent.

The legacy of Pope Paul IV's papacy is thus a complex tapestry, interwoven with threads of doctrinal rigor, political ambition, cultural constraint, and the unyielding pursuit of reform. His drive for purity, however unyielding, was counterbalanced by the widespread repercussions of his policies. This legacy manifested in a profound division between the Church's lofty ideals and its terrestrial exercise of power. In the wake of his reign, critics and reformers alike were compelled to grapple with a sobering truth: that actual authority demands the steadfast defense of core principles and an enduring commitment to mercy, justice, and the open exchange of ideas.

Modern historians, revisiting the archival records, personal letters, satirical engravings, and legal documents from this turbulent period, debate the efficacy and morality of Paul IV's decrees. Some argue that his uncompromising stance was a necessary bulwark against the spread of heresy; others contend that the intolerant measures he employed only deepened social fractures and stifled progress. This ongoing dialogue is a testament to the enduring relevance of his reign—a reminder that the proper exercise of power must constantly walk the fine line between the defense of tradition and the imperative for human dignity.

Reflecting on this turbulent chapter of Church history, one is left with a complex but instructive portrait of an institution struggling to reconcile religious zeal with pragmatic governance. The harsh decrees of Pope Paul IV, while intended to fortify the Church against internal and external threats, inadvertently sowed the seeds of alienation and dissent that would later spur comprehensive reforms. His legacy—etched in stern edicts, ignominious trials, and the whispered laments of a beleaguered populace—remains a powerful lesson for all who wield authority. It underscores a fundamental truth: Pursuing doctrinal purity, when executed without compassion and account-ability, can undermine the very foundations of moral leadership.

Chapter Thirteen

Science Silenced – Pope Urban VIII & the Galileo Affair (1623–1644)

The Scientific Revolution of the seventeenth century arrived like a tidal wave, washing over a Europe steeped in tradition and dogma. In its wake, centuries-old assumptions about the cosmos were violently upended by new methods of observation, measurement, and experimentation. The ancient geocentric model—so long held as self-evident—began to crumble before the penetrating lens of telescopes and the rigorous dissection of mathematical analysis. In this tumultuous environment, the Catholic Church, guardian of spiritual truth for nearly a millennium, found its authority directly challenged. It was during the papacy of Urban VIII (1623–1644) that the dramatic saga of Galileo Galilei unfolded—a conflict that forever altered the relationship between faith and reason.

Urban VIII was a product of his time—a cultured patron of the arts, schooled in the humanistic revival, and a fervent defender of traditional doctrine. He believed that the Church's long-held teachings held divine inspiration and were essential for the proper ordering of society. During his reign, intellectual cultivation and resolute conservatism coexisted in an era when the boundaries of acceptable thought were hotly contested amidst complex political, theological, and artistic forces. Galileo's revolutionary discoveries in this charged atmosphere provided an incendiary challenge to the established cosmic order. With his improved telescope, Galileo beheld the rugged surface of the Moon, discerning craters and mountains long denied by the polished, celestial perfection of Aristotelian heavens. His discovery of the four largest moons orbiting Jupiter shattered the dogma that all celestial bodies must orbit the Earth and hinted at a universe governed by universal laws. His Sidereus Nuncius (Starry Messenger) publication in 1610 electrified the scholarly world and ignited fervent debates in academies and public squares throughout Europe, prompting a radical rethinking of humanity's place in the cosmos.

Galileo's work was liberatory for many in the scientific community, a revelation that the universe adhered to consistent, discoverable laws. Mathematicians and natural philosophers began to question the veracity of a cosmos centered on Earth, and evidence steadily favored the heliocentric model initially proposed by Copernicus. Nevertheless, for the Church, Galileo's assertions posed an existential threat. Urban VIII, long a champion of a geocentric view rooted in theological tradition, was caught in a profound dilemma. Although his refined sensibilities and patronage of the arts might have fostered an environment receptive to new ideas, his duty to uphold doctrine demanded that he preserve the sacred interpretation of Scripture. By displacing humanity from its central position in the divine plan, the heliocentric model challenged the very foundation of Church authority and its established cosmic order.

Misgivings about potential heresy fueled a climate of intense suspicion. The pope and his advisors perceived Galileo's enthusiastic promotion of heliocentric theory not merely as an academic dispute but as a direct affront to the temporal and spiritual power of the Church. Urban VIII sought to stamp out what he viewed as reckless speculation through a series of official decrees and condemnatory pronouncements. Galileo's Dialogue Concerning the Two Chief World Systems, which presented a layered argument subtly endorsing heliocentrism, was met with censure, and he was ultimately forced to recant his views. Summoned to Rome, Galileo faced a tribunal of inquisitors whose secretive proceedings became less an earnest pursuit of truth than an exercise in dogmatic enforcement. Under mounting pressure and likely threats of severe punishment,

Galileo was coerced into recanting his support for the heliocentric model. The whispered defiance, "E pur si move" ("And yet, it moves"), though possibly apocryphal, has come to symbolize the persistence of scientific truth in the face of oppressive authority. This event marked a turning point in the history of science—a stark signal that the sacred authority of the Church was willing to sacrifice intellectual inquiry to maintain its doctrinal imperatives.

The reverberations of the Galileo affair extended far beyond theological debates. The advent of the printing press ensured that both support for and criticism of the Church's stance spread rapidly. Pamphlets, treatises, and satirical engravings proliferated throughout Europe, intensifying public scrutiny and fostering a climate of bitter speculation. In salons in Florence, universities in Padua, and even remote villages, conversations shifted from blind reverence for ancient authority to vibrant dialogues about the nature of truth and the role of religious institutions in the pursuit of knowledge. Urban VIII's condemnation inadvertently laid the groundwork for a transformative reassessment of the relationship between faith and reason. His rigid defense of an outdated cosmic order highlighted emerging shifts in natural philosophy and catalyzed an evolution from Aristotelian dogma to empiricism grounded in observation and experimentation. Galileo's practices—meticulous measurement, systematic observation, and mathematical analysis—gradually gained acceptance as the

bedrock of modern inquiry and ultimately led to the establishment
of the scientific method.

Chapter Fourteen

Struggling with Modernity – Pope Pius IX's Turbulent Reforms (1846–1878)

The mid-nineteenth century marked an era of dramatic transformation in Europe as liberalism, nationalism, industrialization, and scientific innovation reshaped societies that had long been steeped in tradition and dogma. Against this backdrop of rapid change, few pontificates were as polarizing or as transformative as that of Pope Pius IX, whose lengthy reign from 1846 until 1878 became a crucible in which the old world of ecclesiastical authority collided head-on with the emerging forces of modernity. His papacy was defined by dramatic declarations and tumultuous reforms that fortified the Church's longstanding doctrines and alienated many of its followers, setting the stage for ongoing struggles in reconciling faith with an increasingly liberal and secular society.

From the very early years of his rule, Pius IX sought to reassert the Church's role as the unchallengeable guardian of divine truth when modern ideas were rapidly questioning traditional certainties. One of his most defining moments was his proclamation of papal infallibility during the First Vatican Council. This dogmatic decree, intended as a theological and political bulwark, was meant to reinforce the pope's absolute authority over faith and morals. His supporters saw this as an essential measure to preserve centuries-old doctrines in an age dominated by the rationalism of the Enlightenment and the critical spirit of liberalism. However, the declaration was met with fierce opposition from many circles that viewed it as a rigid assertion of control, emblematic of a conservatism increasingly at odds with progressive ideas about individual liberty and democratic participation.

In confronting modernity, Pius IX adopted internal measures designed to solidify Church authority even as external forces challenged its temporal power. He reformed the administrative structures of the Vatican, standardizing liturgical practices and instituting strict disciplinary measures among the clergy. His reforms were intended to stamp out inefficiencies and any remnants of what he saw as moral laxity—a necessary step, he believed, to restore the Church's stature in the face of secular criticism. Nevertheless, by imposing such rigid uniformity, these reforms also curtailed intellectual freedom within the Church and contributed to an atmosphere of inquisition rather than inspiration. Many theologians and educators found themselves caught between the need to adhere to dogmatic prescriptions and the desire to engage with the new ideas emerging from the advances in science, philosophy, and political theory.

The external pressures facing Pius IX were as formidable as those within the Church. Italy, in particular, was undergoing massive changes as the Risorgimento—a movement for Italian unification—challenged the centuries-old temporal power held by the Papal States. The gradual erosion of papal territory, climaxing in the capture of Rome in the 1870s and the annexation of the Papal States into a modern nation-state, was not only a political catastrophe but a profound symbolic blow to the Church's claim to divine sovereignty. Nationalist fervor and the demands for representative government swept across the continent, and liberal political reform was no longer confined to academic discourse; it had become a rallying cry for those who sought an end to the old feudal order. In this volatile climate, Pius IX's rejection of liberal reforms—while intended to be a safeguard against what he perceived as moral decay—only deepened the gap between the Church and the evolving aspirations of modern society.

Technological progress also played an unexpected role in reshaping the landscape during his papacy. The advent of the telegraph, the proliferation of newspapers, and the spread of mass-printed journals enabled the rapid circulation of ideas and criticisms. News of the Church's rigid policies, its resistance to reform, and the dramatic events unfolding during the Italian unification reached an ever-wider audience than ever before. Pamphlets and essays, both in support of and against his policies, fueled public debate and laid the ground-work for a more informed—and increasingly critical—citizenry. This newfound transparency, combined with the increasing literacy rates of the era, accelerated the erosion of the previously unassailable aura of ecclesiastical authority.

Amid these accelerations of modernity, the intellectual transfor-mation during this period was profound. The fallout from revolu-tionary episodes such as the Galileo affair had already set in motion an epistemological shift, moving the basis of knowledge away from unquestioned ancient authority toward a methodology rooted in empirical observation and reason. Amid these dynamics, thinkers within and outside the Church began questioning the insistence on blind obedience to tradition. Scholars debated vigorously whether faith must necessarily be tethered to all aspects of doctrinal rigidity or whether it could evolve by integrating the insights gleaned from sci-entific and philosophical inquiry. The emergence of a more critical, investigatory approach in universities and public discourse foreshadowed a long-term intellectual reformation. This reformation was to be echoed in the cathartic debates of the late nineteenth century.

At the heart of Pius IX's struggle with modernity lies a profoundly human story—a narrative marked by his anxieties and internal conflicts. His private correspondence, preserved in meticulous detail in Church archives, reveals a man tormented by the rapid pace of change that threatened to render the traditions he had devoted his life to protecting into obsolescence. In one letter, written in a tone of melancholic introspection, he lamented the erosion of moral certainties that had once defined European society. His words betray an inner turmoil: a mixture of despair over losing a long-cherished order and a steely determination to hold back the tide of liberal reforms. This personal dimension, too often overshadowed by doctrinal debates and political struggles, offers a window into the loneliness and isolation of a pope who felt himself to be the last guardian of a fading era.

Within the Church, these tensions were manifested as deep-seated divisions. While ardent traditionalists rallied around Pius IX as a symbol of unyielding faith and continuity, a growing number of younger Catholics and progressive intellectuals viewed his policies as anachronistic and counterproductive. Academic reforms were slow to take hold, and in many seminaries, the strains between the demands of modern scientific inquiry and the rigid enforcement of doctrinal orthodoxy led to disagreements that threatened to split the body of the faithful. This internal schism was further compounded by external criticisms from European liberals and rationalists, who argued that the Church's insistence on an immutable doctrine not only stifled creativity and change but also alienated many of its adherents from a faith that could engage meaningfully with the modern world.

The political consequences of his reign were equally far-reaching. As nation-states emerged from the old feudal mosaic, many political leaders seized upon the Church's perceived conservatism as a pretext for reducing its influence in public affairs. In Italy, the nationalist movement that ultimately led to the country's unification argued that an institution so rigidly opposed to reform could no longer serve as the moral compass of a modern society. The loss of the Papal States, symbolizing the final capitulation of temporal power to the forces of liberal nationalism, left an indelible mark on the psyche of the Church. This political isolation would not vanish overnight but instead set in motion a series of reforms and dialogues in later decades that sought to reconcile the Church's ancient traditions with the aspirations of a modern state.

The cultural impact of these events was equally transformative. Artistic and literary circles across Europe were abuzz with responses to the tumult of the mid-nineteenth century—responses that ranged from overt praise of the Church's steadfastness to caustic satire aimed squarely at its resistance to change. Artists depicted Pius IX as both an infallible religious leader and a tragic figure caught in a relentless battle between the old order and the inexorable march of progress. Satirical engravings and biting literary works captured the irony of a pope who, in his fervor to preserve tradition, inadvertently accelerated the demise of the institution he sought to defend. These cultural artifacts provided a poignant commentary on the evolving relationship between faith and modernity—a dialogue that remains central to our understanding of the period.

In evaluating the long-term ramifications of his tumultuous reforms, modern scholars continue to grapple with the dual legacy of Pius IX. On one side, his unwavering commitment to Catholic orthodoxy and bold declarations, such as the dogma of papal infallibility, helped establish a clear boundary between sacred doctrine and secular innovation. On the other hand, his staunch resistance to the liberal reforms of his time, along with his failure to engage constructively with the burgeoning ideas of democracy and scientific progress, tarnished his reputation among future generations. This contentious legacy contributed to an enduring debate about the proper role of religion in an era increasingly defined by rational inquiry and public accountability. This debate reverberates in modern discussions on the separation of Church and state and the need for an adaptable, forward-looking faith.

With all its passionate declarations and hardline policies, the era of Pius IX ultimately set the stage for the modern Catholic Church's gradual transition toward a more dialogical posture. In the decades that followed his papacy, voices within the Church began calling for a more nuanced understanding of tradition—one that would allow the Church to remain relevant in a world characterized by rapid change and ideological pluralism. Although these calls for reform would evolve slowly and sometimes painfully, they signaled the beginning of a long-term renewal process that continues to shape how the Church interacts with modern society. The legacy of Pius IX thus serves as a potent reminder that the struggle between unyielding conservatism and progressive reform is a perennial one—a struggle that demands both resolve and, ultimately, the courage to embrace change without abandoning core principles.

Adding further texture to this multifaceted narrative are the numerous primary sources documenting the era—meticulous records of official decrees, heartfelt personal letters of influential clerics, and the vivid accounts of contemporary critics who witnessed the transformative events unfold. These sources paint a rich and complex picture of an age defined by upheaval, offering insights into the legal and political maneuvers of a pontiff determined to hold the line against modernity and into the emotional and psychological toll exacted on both leaders and laypeople. Through these documents, one can trace the gradual erosion of authority that began with defiant papal proclamations and culminated in a society where democratic ideals and scientific inquiry were afforded increasing legitimacy.

In the final synthesis, the papacy of Pope Pius IX encapsulates the multifarious struggle of an institution confronting the full force of modernity. His reforms, designed to preserve a long-cherished religious doctrine, were simultaneously a desperate bid to assert timeless authority amid the clamor for change. Nevertheless, while his measures may have fortified the Church's institutional framework, they also underscored the challenges of maintaining spiritual relevance in a rapidly evolving world. The complex interplay between tradition and progress during his reign laid the groundwork for subsequent debates about the nature of authority, the role of religious institutions in public life, and the capacity for reform when confronted with the relentless demands of modernization.

Ultimately, the legacy of Pope Pius IX endures as a profound source of reflection on the delicate balance between the preservation of sacred tradition and the imperative for social and intellectual renewal. His reign, replete with icy proclamations and a fervent resistance to change, invites modern readers to examine how institutions—no matter how venerable—must continually adapt to remain relevant in an ever-changing world. The turbulent years of his papacy serve as both a testament to the enduring power of faith and a cautionary tale about the dangers of resisting progress. For those who seek to understand the evolution of modernity in the context of religious history, the story of Pius IX offers timeless lessons about the interplay of politics, culture, technology, and personal conviction. This legacy continues to inspire and challenge us to reconcile the past with the promise of the future.

Chapter Fifteen

The Face of War – Pope Benedict XV in World War I (1914–1922)

The devastation of World War I reshaped the very fabric of global civilization, leaving nation-states, communities, and individuals alike deeply scarred by the horrors of modern warfare. In this era of relentless mechanized violence and unprecedented political upheaval, Pope Benedict XV ascended to the papal throne in 1914, assuming leadership when the old certainties were dissolving amid the roar of artillery and the cries of a suffering populace. His pontificate, stretching until 1922, unfolded in a profound moral crisis—when traditional notions of national loyalty, religious doctrine, and human compassion were being forcefully renegotiated. Facing an international conflict marked not only by massive casualties on the battlefield but also by the systematic targeting of civilian populations, Benedict XV found himself compelled to extend his responsibilities far beyond spiritual guidance. In addition to tending to the souls of the faithful, he assumed the mantle of an international mediator, reaching out to belligerents with heartfelt appeals for peace and reconciliation.

From the onset of the war, Benedict XV demonstrated an unwavering commitment to the cause of peace. In a series of meticulously drafted letters and impassioned public addresses, he implored the leaders of warring nations to seek a negotiated settlement—emphasizing that the actual cost of the conflict was measured not in territorial gains nor fleeting political victories but in the endless suffering of innocents. His communications, disseminated through official channels and printed widely in newspapers and pamphlets, painted a picture of a world teetering on the brink of annihilation. The pope's language was eloquent and deeply compassionate, resonating with the grief of nations battered by endless loss. Nevertheless, for all his earnest appeals, his cautious, deliberate diplomacy was met with skepticism by many political and military leaders, many of whom dismissed his interventions as naïve in the face of entrenched nationalistic ambitions. Even so, his repeated entreaties gradually contributed to an international atmosphere where dialogue, however tentative—began to supplement the clamor for total war.

Benedict XV's diplomatic initiatives were multifaceted. On one level, he reached out directly to heads of state, issuing carefully worded missives that proposed detailed plans for cease-fires, establishing humanitarian corridors, and the organization of neutral peace conferences. These proposals were neither impulsive nor ideologically extreme; instead, they were underpinned by a pragmatic assessment of military realities and the moral imperative to protect noncombatants. Numerous contemporary records—intercepted telegrams, diplomatic memoirs, and memoirs of delegates at informal peace talks—document his tireless efforts to bridge the gap between warring factions. Although these overtures rarely produced immediate results, over time, they contributed to the gradual emergence of a post-war international order in which the idea of collective security took root. His vision of a supranational dialogue, one that transcended national borders and rivalries, anticipated later institutions such as the League of Nations and, eventually, the United Nations.

Beyond his high-level diplomatic endeavors, the personal and psychological dimensions of Benedict XV's wartime papacy offers a vivid portrait of leadership under duress. The pope penned numerous reflective memoranda and letters in the solitude of his private study, away from the relentless scrutiny of the press and the demands of ever-shifting political alliances. These documents, preserved with painstaking care in the Vatican archives, reveal a man deeply troubled by the scale and inhumanity of the conflict. He described sleepless nights spent haunted by images of devastated towns, heart-wrenching accounts of families torn apart, and the overwhelming burden of responsibility for a world in crisis. In one particularly poignant letter addressed to a close confidant, he sorrowfully noted that every new report of civilian suffering etched a fresh line of grief upon his soul—a sentiment that encapsulated both his empathy for the victims and his profound feeling of impotence in the face of overwhelming state power. This internal torment, the culmination of personal sacrifice and the crushing loneliness of moral leadership, rendered his public pronouncements all the more resonant, transforming them into quiet pleas for humanity amidst the cacophony of war.

The broader international context of Benedict XV's papacy was marked by rapid technological and social changes that further complicated his mission. The war itself, often characterized as the first "total war," mobilized entire societies through advancements in communication and transportation—telegraphs transmitted urgent appeals across continents. At the same time, mass-produced newspapers and magazines disseminated both news and propaganda with unprecedented speed. This greater access to information meant that the pope's messages for peace were heard not only by power brokers and political elites but also by an increasingly literate and politically engaged global citizenry. The rapid circulation of ideas contributed to a burgeoning international debate over warfare ethics and political power responsibilities. In this vibrant atmosphere of controversy,

Benedict XV's cautious diplomacy, while criticized by hardliners as insufficient—later emerged as an early, if imperfect, steppingstone toward establishing international humanitarian law. His persistent insistence on protecting noncombatants and advocating for the humane treatment of prisoners provided, for many future policymakers, ethical guidelines that would ultimately influence the formulation of the Geneva Conventions and other frameworks of wartime conduct.

Culturally, the impact of Benedict XV's papacy during World War I permeated every stratum of society. In the arts, juxtaposing his placid, compassionate persona with the devastation of modern warfare spurred a rich vein of creative output: writers, painters, and musicians found in his appeals both inspiration and a call to action. Poets composed elegies mourning the loss of hope, while playwrights and novelists crafted narratives that dramatized the complex interplay between divine mercy and human folly. In the post-war years, Galleries and public exhibitions often featured works depicting the pope as a solitary beacon of calm—a figure of light calling out against the darkness of desolation. These cultural expressions not only commemorated his efforts to mediate the horrors of war but also served to humanize a conflict otherwise characterized by its ruthless mechanization.

Critics of Benedict XV's approach argued that his measured stance, though morally sound, amounted to passive condolence rather than the hard political action needed to end hostilities decisively. Many military leaders and nationalist ideologues decried his calls for neutrality, arguing that his interventions risked undermining the resolve of their armies. However, contemporaneous sources also reveal that countless ordinary citizens, traumatized by the endless cycle of violence, took solace in his moral leadership. For them, the pope's recurring messages of peace and reconciliation offered a counterpoint to the destructive fervor of nationalism. His appeals fostered a nascent international sentiment, a shared awareness that common humanity could and must prevail even amidst the most brutal conflicts.

The legacy of Pope Benedict XV in World War I is inherently multifaceted. His efforts, though containing elements of cautious diplomacy that did not immediately halt the war's momentum, nevertheless laid crucial groundwork for the later rethinking of international conflict resolution. His persistent emphasis on humanitarian considerations—on the idea that even amid violence, the dignity of every human life was sacrosanct—resonated deeply in the post-war era. In many respects, his initiatives to create safer humanitarian corridors, proposals for hospital exchange programs, and repeated calls for a pause in the relentless advance of mechanized destruction were precursors to the moral frameworks underpinning modern international law.

In examining the personal dimensions of his wartime papacy, one is struck by the duality of his existence—a leader whose public persona of serene compassion conceals a private world of intense sorrow, isolation, and, ultimately, unwavering resolve. His recorded reflections reveal a man profoundly conscious of the immense duties that weighed upon him. Nevertheless, amidst the relentless pummeling of modernity, he remained steadfast, continuously advocating for peace in a world that seemed determined to descend into chaos. These intimate glimpses into his internal struggles enrich our understanding of his character and underscore the inescapable fact that moral leadership in times of war comes at a steep personal price.

Throughout the tumult of global conflict, the international ripple effects of Benedict XV's peace efforts contributed to the slow but eventual establishment of a post-war international order. Although his diplomatic overtures were insufficient to end the war, they helped cultivate a spirit of multinational dialogue prelude to the later creation of institutions designed to foster global cooperation and prevent future conflicts. Thus, His legacy extends beyond the immediate historical moment, inviting future generations to reflect on the ethical imperatives underpinning modern diplomacy. The notion that the horrors of war necessitate a robust and compassionate international community has become a central tenet of subsequent peacekeeping endeavors. It continues to inform debates over the role of global institutions in today's conflicts.

Ultimately, the legacy of Pope Benedict XV as "The Face of War" during World War I is a profound, multi-dimensional narrative—a chronicle of moral courage and compassionate diplomacy played out against the backdrop of modern mechanized warfare. His papacy, defined by a constant, if constrained, determination to mediate in an era of relentless violence, stands as a testament to the resilience of the human spirit. In his appeals for peace, cautious yet persistent diplomatic endeavors, and sacrifices, one finds an enduring reminder that even amidst the tumult of war, the aspirations for reconciliation and the preservation of human dignity must never be abandoned.

For modern readers, the story of Benedict XV's wartime papacy offers both inspiration and a sobering lesson. It reveals that pursuing peace in a modern, fragmented world requires not just the articulation of lofty ideals but also pragmatic, courageous action—a delicate balance between compassion and the implacable realities of state power. As the international community today continues to grapple with the challenges of global conflict and the ethical dilemmas posed by modern warfare, the legacy of Benedict XV remains a beacon, urging us to remember that the call for peace, though fraught with sacrifice and compromise, is inevitably the noblest endeavor of human leadership.

Thus, the extraordinary narrative of Pope Benedict XV during World War I, with its rich tapestry of diplomatic initiative, personal torment, and cultural impact, is a testament to the resilience of the human spirit and a call to action for all who believe in the possibility of peace. In the echo of every cease-fire call and every humanitarian plea, his enduring legacy challenges each generation to strive for a world where the horrors of conflict are supplanted by the enduring hope of reconciliation and in which the sanctity of human life remains inviolable.

Chapter Sixteen

Diplomacy Under Fire – Pope Pius XI and Nazi Germany (1922–1939)

The interwar years were marked by an undercurrent of political extremism and the inexorable rise of totalitarian regimes. For Pope Pius XI, whose pontificate spanned from 1922 until 1939, these decades presented a formidable diplomatic challenge: how to safeguard the Church's spiritual mission and institutional integrity while operating in an increasingly hostile geopolitical environment. Nowhere was this tension more evident than in his dealings with Nazi Germany, the regime that, by the early 1930s, had transformed from a fringe radical movement into a potent threat to Europe's moral and political order.

From his ascension in 1922, Pius XI inherited a Europe in flux—one still grappling with the wounds of World War I and witnessing the emergence of new nationalistic fervor. At first, the Vatican sought a measured dialogue with the new political forces; however, as the Nazi Party steadily gained power and its brutal policies became evident, the pope found himself forced to walk a treacherous diplomatic tightrope. Having long enjoyed a privileged position in European society, the Church suddenly had to confront the sobering reality that traditional safeguards were under siege. Eager to consolidate their ideological control, German leaders saw the Church's influence as both a potential threat and a tool to co-opt ordinary citizens. Thus, from the early 1930s onward, the Vatican increasingly recognized that a distinct strategy would be necessary to preserve the spiritual autonomy of the Catholic faithful.

In 1933, an agreement was forged that would come to epitomize the complex and often contentious relationship between the Holy See and the Nazi regime: the Reichskonkordat. On its face, this concordat was a diplomatic triumph. This treaty ostensibly guaranteed the Church's operational freedom, property rights, and the ability to continue teaching Catholic doctrine without interference. For Pope Pius XI and his diplomats, the Reichskonkordat was seen as a necessary safeguard against rampant anti-Church measures. It was hoped that by binding the Nazi government to certain formal obligations, the Church could maintain a foothold in a society increasingly stirred by extremist ideologies.

Nevertheless, such hopes were soon dashed. Almost immediately after its ratification, the Nazi regime began to breach the terms of the concordat with alarming regularity. The government's insidious censorship, the erosion of religious freedoms, and the systematic persecution of dissenters—all occurred under the protective shadow of the treaty. Behind closed doors, the pontiff and his advisors were forced to confront the bitter truth that the Reichskonkordat, rather than shielding the Church, had become a double-edged sword, one with which the Nazi state fashioned a veneer of legitimacy. In secret diplomatic cables and carefully archived communications, high-ranking Vatican officials lamented the abuse of the pact, noting that every violation chipped away at the Church's credibility. In private, Pius XI wrestled with the moral ambiguity of the accord; to what extent had the Church compromised its eternal principles by agreeing to terms with a regime whose ideology was antithetical to the Church's teachings on human dignity and love?

The public response to the Reichskonkordat was a tempest of contradictions. Reassured by even the faintest chance of normalcy, Conservative Catholics initially welcomed the treaty as a bulwark against secular assaults. Meanwhile, progressive voices within and outside the Church decried the agreement as a capitulation to Nazi power. In newspapers, academic treatises, and heated discussions in European salons, critics argued that any diplomatic arrangement with such a regime risked sliding the Church down a slippery slope toward moral complicity. The findings of later historical analyses would show that the Reichskonkordat played a pragmatic, if conflicted, role in the political maneuverings of the era—providing the Nazi state with a tool for social control while simultaneously leaving the Church exposed to moral criticism.

As the 1930s advanced, the true nature of Nazi racial policies and the regime's systematic persecution of Jews, political dissenters, and other marginalized groups became ever more apparent. Confronted with these grim realities, Pope Pius XI was compelled to articulate a voice of moral outrage that diplomatic niceties could no longer suppress. This resolve manifested most notably in the encyclical Mit Brennender Sorge ("With Burning Concern"), a document that, though shrouded in delicate language to avoid immediate diplomatic repercussions, offered a piercing censure of the Nazi regime's ideological excesses. Smuggled into Germany in defiance of state restrictions and read aloud from pulpits nationwide, Mit Brennender Sorge was a masterful act of subversive communication. Its carefully chosen phrases condemned the distortion of Christian truths, denounced the dehumanizing racial policies, and called upon German Catholics to resist the seductive lure of totalitarian conquests. The encyclical's impact rippled through Germany and beyond—it galvanized local resistance, reawakened dormant voices of opposition, and forever altered the moral landscape of the era.

Behind the public pronouncements lay an intricate web of diplomatic negotiations and confidential exchanges. In the shadowy corridors of the Vatican, emissaries engaged in covert dialogues with representatives from both sympathetic and antagonistic regimes. These negotiations were fraught with peril; every coded telegram, every intercepted memorandum, and every hushed conversation was an exercise in moral and political balance. The pope's hidden correspondences reveal a leader acutely aware that overt hostility could jeopardize clandestine humanitarian initiatives to save innocent lives. There are accounts of secret rescue operations—efforts organized through back channels that provided sanctuary to Jews and political refugees persecuted by the Nazi state. While scholars continue to debate the precise scope and efficacy of these covert operations, the archival evidence underscores the desperate measures taken by the Vatican to alleviate the suffering wrought by ideological tyranny.

In parallel with these diplomatic struggles, the internal atmosphere within the Church was one of profound tension and introspection. Senior clerics, theologians, and lay advisors wrestled with the ethical dilemmas of an increasingly violent political landscape. Within the hallowed offices of the Secretariat of State, debates flared over the moral responsibilities of the Church in the face of overwhelming injustice. Some argued for a more outspoken denunciation of Nazi atrocities—a forceful break with the appeasement policies of previous years. Others maintained that a discreet, cautious approach was the only viable means of preserving the Church's capacity to operate amidst the chaos of war. These internal deliberations, recorded in long-forgotten meeting minutes and private letters, paint a picture of a leadership caught between idealism and pragmatism, between an unyielding commitment to eternal truth and the crushing necessity of political survival.

The cultural reverberations of Pope Pius XI's struggle with Nazi Germany were profound and deeply symbolic. Across Europe, intellectuals and artists responded to the papal pronouncements with admiration, sorrow, and defiant resistance. In theaters and cafés, plays and poems emerged that depicted a solitary pontiff, shrouded in mystery, standing as a lone sentinel against the advance of darkness. Illustrators and muralists fashioned images of the pope as a luminous figure—his serene face illuminated by the flame of divine righteousness—even as the backdrop of war-torn landscapes and shattered lives provided a stark reminder of the real cost of totalitarian power. These cultural expressions, often produced in clandestine settings to evade censorship, helped cement Pius XI as a symbolic leader whose moral courage was memorialized in doctrinal texts and the living art of popular memory.

Technological advancements during this era played an unexpected role in further magnifying the Vatican's strategic dilemmas and public profile. The proliferation of radio broadcasts, mass-circulated newspapers, and the rapid transmission of telegraphs ensured that the pope's messages reached an unprecedented global audience. However, this immediacy of communication often transformed nuanced diplomatic statements into incendiary headlines, amplifying both the acclaim and the criticism the Church faced. In a world where every action was scrutinized in near real-time, even a single ill-chosen word could symbolize broader failures in moral leadership. Modern reexaminations of this phenomenon reveal that the rapid flow of information energized the international discourse on human rights and, paradoxically, accelerated the rate at which Church policies were questioned and judged by a hyper-informed public.

The legacy of Pope Pius XI's diplomacy with Nazi Germany has continued to be a subject of intense debate among historians, theologians, and political theorists. Some contend that his cautious, discreet measures were the best possible response given the unyielding power of the Nazi regime; others argue that his inability—or unwillingness—to mount a more vociferous public condemnation ultimately compromised the moral authority of the Church. Regardless of one's perspective, it is clear that his tenure, at its core, was a study of the painful calculus of survival during an epoch marked by extremes. The enduring importance of his diplomatic decisions is reflected in the post-war evolution of international humanitarian law, the eventual establishment of global human rights standards, and how his legacy has been invoked in subsequent generations as a cautionary tale of moral ambiguity.

Today, the enduring influence of Pope Pius XI's engagement with Nazi Germany remains interwoven with the ideological and ethical challenges that continue to confront international leaders. His story serves as a sober reminder that when totalitarian power is poised to crush the voice of humanity, even a centuries-old institution must grapple with paradoxes that defy clear-cut solutions. The Reichskonkordat and Mit Brennender Sorge endure as emblematic documents—a testament to the complexity of an era when the demands of preserving spiritual integrity and protecting human life collided with the unrelenting pressures of modern statecraft.

In retrospect, the diplomatic efforts of Pope Pius XI during his fraught encounters with Nazi Germany stand as one of the most intricate chapters in the history of moral leadership. His legacy, captured in a vast array of diplomatic cables, private correspondence, and public declarations, challenges us to confront the uncomfortable questions of how best to defend eternal truths in the face of transient yet devastating human cruelty. The moral lessons he imparted—of cautious resolve, the necessity of covert humanitarian action, and the unyielding hold of conscience even under oppressive regimes—continue to inform modern discussions on international ethics and leadership responsibilities.

Thus, the chapter of Pope Pius XI's diplomacy with Nazi Germany from 1922 to 1939 remains a timeless narrative of ambition, compromise, and defiance. This narrative compels each generation to reflect on the enduring struggle between the forces of totalitarianism and the inviolable rights of human dignity. In the dance between secrecy and public denunciation, between cautious negotiation and the call for moral clarity, the legacy of Pius XI invites modern readers to ponder not only the historical costs of political compromise but the ever-relevant imperative to stand for justice even when the road is cloaked in darkness.

Chapter Seventeen

Stepping into Darkness —The Wartime Legacy of Pope Pius XII (1939-1958)

When World War II erupted in September 1939, its arrival plunged the world into a darkness that few had ever imagined—a darkness marked by the relentless pounding of mechanized warfare, the systematic persecution of entire peoples, and a moral disintegration that shook the very foundations of civilization. Amid this global catastrophe, the mantle of spiritual leadership fell to Pope Pius XII. Ascending to the papacy when humanity's certainties were being swept away, he inherited the duty to shepherd millions of faithful souls and the immense challenge of guiding an institution steeped in centuries of tradition through a maelstrom of modern horrors.

From the onset, Pius XII recognized that the unprecedented scale of suffering demanded a response both measured and shrouded in the subtleties of international diplomacy. Adopting a policy of cautious neutrality, he understood that overt political entanglements could endanger the Church's capacity to deliver aid and spiritual solace. Nevertheless, even as he refrained from public denunciations that might provoke further bloodshed, behind closed Vatican doors, the pope's inner world was wracked with anguish. In confidential diaries and secret letters later uncovered in the Vatican archives, he confessed that the reports from the front—tales of mass deportations, unspeakable acts of cruelty, and the mechanized extermination of entire communities—were nightly torments that gnawed at his spirit. "Each report of human loss creates a fissure in my soul, a darkness that even the hope of salvation cannot mend," he wrote in one such entry, words that capture the profound isolation and responsibility he bore during those interminable years.

The nature of modern conflict meant that the face of evil was not always visible on battlefields covered in mud and barbed wire; it was also inscribed in the corridors of power, coded telegrams, and behind layers of diplomatic rhetoric. As the Nazi regime's racial policies and systematic exterminations began to leave an indelible mark on Europe, the Vatican was forced to confront the bitter paradox of remaining neutral while silently combating inhumanity. The Reichskonkordat, signed in 1933, had once promised certain guarantees for the Church in Nazi Germany; however, as the regime flagrantly violated its terms—exploiting the accord to muzzle dissent and further its vile objectives—Pius XII found himself caught in a moral and political labyrinth. His private correspondences reveal a man acutely aware that each concession made for institutional survival risked imperiling the lives of countless innocents. Thus, behind the public façade of silence, the Holy See mobilized an intricate network of covert initiatives, a secret channel that enabled discreet assistance to refugees, safe houses for those fleeing persecution, and financial support for escape networks that defied the tyranny of total war.

This clandestine diplomacy was conducted in a world where every word, every gesture, carried the potential to shift the delicate balance between survival and moral denunciation. In a series of intercepted diplomatic cables and encrypted memoranda that have since come to light, Vatican emissaries detailed their efforts to engage with high-ranking officials in neutral countries and even within the very regimes that perpetrated war's atrocities. The pope's representatives needed to craft messages firm enough to convey moral disapproval yet ambiguous enough to allow continued dialogue with powers whose approval was sometimes essential for saving lives. Ambition and fear, opportunity and peril—all these forces converged in the

Vatican's secret negotiations, where the fate of millions often hung on the careful calibration of a single, unpublicized communiqué.

Within this precarious context, the cultural impact of Pius XII's wartime papacy was profound. Throughout Europe, as radio transmissions crackled with news of overwhelming loss and newspapers splashed sensational headlines across cities, the Church's moral pronouncements became a touchstone for a weary public searching for hope. In bombed-out basements turned into impromptu meeting halls, refugees and civilians alike clung to accounts of the pope's assurances that an unwavering commitment to human dignity lay beneath the veneer of geopolitical maneuvering. In one remarkable episode, a small village in occupied Poland recalled the story of its local priest receiving a secretly transmitted letter from the Vatican instructing him to organize a clandestine clinic to care for children injured by aerial bombardments. Such narratives, passed down through generations, imbued the abstract rhetoric of Vatican diplomacy with tangible hope—a hope that even amid the relentless machinery of state-sponsored violence, compassion could weave a fragile thread of survival.

At the same time, the rapid advancements in technology during the war played a double role in shaping public perception and the effectiveness of the Vatican's covert operations. The telegraph and radio broke down distance barriers, transmitting the pope's measured

messages of condolence and hope to a global audience. Mass-produced newspapers and clandestine pamphlets reached millions, ensuring his moral voice was heard far and wide while the Church's
high-level diplomacy was veiled in secrecy. Nevertheless, this same
multiplicity of communication channels also magnified criticism,
as journalists and dissidents scrutinized the apparent silence of the
papal office over specific atrocities. Debates erupted in intellectual
salons and in the emerging realms of broadcast media, where the
moral charges against both the Nazi and Fascist powers—and even
against the cautious measures of the Church—were laid bare for
all to hear. This dynamic interplay of public and private discourse
distills the era's intense political and moral complexities into a vivid
narrative of human suffering, resilience, and the enduring quest for
justice.

Beyond the public record and the pages of official documents,
the personal dimension of Pope Pius XII's wartime legacy adds an
especially poignant texture to the story. In rare, intimate reflections
penned in the secrecy of his private study, the pope revealed a man
tormented by the endless litany of human misery. In one such journal
entry, he described the nights when sleep would not come, as his
imagination became haunted by the faces of those lost in the horror
of systematic violence—a montage of grief and hopelessness that
no earthly solace could soothe. His private utterances—erroneously

dismissed by some as the resignation of a leader overwhelmed by force—suggest instead a quiet, steadfast resolve to bear the burden of moral responsibility despite the personal anguish it entailed. This human vulnerability, so infrequently glimpsed by the public world, endears the pope's legacy to many and serves as a reminder that even the most powerful figures are not immune to the tragic consequences of inhumanity.

In parallel with these covert humanitarian efforts, Pope Pius XII navigated the treacherous waters of a divided international stage. The diplomatic legacy of his papacy is a study in contrasts—a balancing act executed under extraordinary pressure. Public pronouncements maintained a veneer of neutrality, while private channels pulsed with intensive negotiations intended to de-escalate localized conflicts. His emissaries, operating under the constant threat of reprisals by totalitarian regimes, marshaled their modest resources and reported every small victory in protocols that later played a crucial role in shaping post-war humanitarian frameworks. Those unwavering efforts eventually helped to lay the groundwork for the Geneva Conventions and subsequent international legal instruments designed to protect vulnerable populations in times of armed conflict. Though they did not stop the war, the complex web of agreements and moral pleas crafted during those years contributed incrementally to the internationalization of ethical norms that persist today.

The era's cultural landscape bore unmistakable traces of the papacy's quiet, determined intervention. In the aftermath of the war, the memory of those years emerged in stirring artistic expressions and literary works that modeled the figure of Pope Pius XII as a solitary guardian of humanity. In the smoky backroom discussions of post-war intellectuals, as well as on the canvases of painters and in the verses of poets, the pope was simultaneously celebrated as a tragic hero and critiqued as a symbol of morally compromised silence. Subterranean theater performances in ruined city squares depicted an austere figure cloaked in papal vestments, walking alone through devastated landscapes, an allegory of hope and sorrow intertwined. Such cultural portrayals reinforced the idea that leadership in the face of overwhelming adversity is as much about bearing witness to tragedy as it is about inspiring the courage to reclaim lost hope.

With the outbreak of the Cold War shortly after the conclusion of World War II, the legacy of Pope Pius XII's wartime tenure continued to resonate in new geopolitical configurations. As rival superpowers emerged to contest new spheres of influence, those who witnessed his discreet interventions recalled his measured diplomacy as a harbinger of the delicate balance between state power and moral responsibility. The lessons embedded in his secret correspondences and quietly transmitted messages—recorded now in exhaustive Vatican archives—offered a framework for understanding that even in the darkest moments, pursuing justice demands unwavering ethical resolve and the willingness to employ subtle, sometimes ambiguous, negotiation channels.

The enduring enigma of Pope Pius XII's actions during the war and the multifaceted legacy he left behind remains a subject of intense scrutiny and debate among historians, theologians, and political philosophers. Some contend that his cautious approach, borne out of informed prudence, allowed the Church to emerge as a vital, if conflicted, actor in the post-war reconstruction of international order. Others argue that his silence on specific atrocities—and the compromises implied by his initial treaties—has forever tarnished his record. What remains undeniable, however, is that his papacy during this period encapsulated the agonizing tension between the demands of sheer survival and the imperatives of moral duty. This tension continues to illuminate the challenges leaders face in times of global crisis.

As we reflect on this period—on the endless diplomatic cables, the hushed meetings, the private laments etched in secret diaries, and the epic struggles unfolding on public stages—we come to appreciate that the legacy of Pope Pius XII is not easily compartmentalized into triumph or failure. Instead, it is a mosaic of blurred lines, quiet heroism, and agonizing choices that forced one of the world's most ancient institutions into the darkness of modern warfare. In doing so, he left us with a legacy that challenges us to examine statecraft's ethical dimensions, moral leadership's responsibilities, and the enduring human capacity for compassion, even under the most adverse conditions.

In the end, the wartime legacy of Pope Pius XII stands as a somber yet compelling chapter in the annals of moral leadership. The narrative invites us to confront the deep contradictions of an age when silence, speech, secrecy, transparency, compassion, and pragmatism coexisted in a fragile equilibrium. His story calls upon each generation to consider how best to act when faced with seemingly insurmountable darkness. This call resonates with undiminished urgency over seventy years after he died in 1958. The legacy of Pope Pius XII challenges us to keep alive the hope that even in the shadow of modern totalitarianism, the unyielding light of moral courage can guide humanity toward a future defined by justice, mercy, and an enduring commitment to human dignity.

Chapter Eighteen

Faith in a Changed World – Pope Paul VI and Modern Morality (1963–1978)

The world that Pope Paul VI inherited in 1963 was one of unprecedented dynamism—a postwar era defined by sweeping technological advances, explosive social movements, and a deep questioning of traditional values. In the wake of the Second Vatican Council's transformative declarations, the Catholic Church was newly called upon to engage with modernity not as a relic of the past but as a living community prepared to dialogue with an evolving cultural landscape. For Paul VI, charged with shepherding a global flock amid the clamor of civil rights movements, sexual liberation, and political upheaval, the challenge was to reimagine what it meant to carry the eternal message of the Gospel into a world that increasingly prized personal freedom and scientific progress.

Immediately upon his accession, Paul VI set about implementing the reforms approved at Vatican II. This transformation was not merely about updating liturgical language but a holistic reawakening. He introduced the vernacular to the liturgy so that scriptural texts and prayers could resonate in the everyday language of the faithful, profoundly altering centuries-old rites that had long been shrouded in Latin. Church buildings that had once echoed with recitations in an ancient tongue suddenly became vibrant centers of community as congregants listened and responded in their own words. In these new celebrations, the sense of mystery inherent in the sacred was preserved even as the pontiff encouraged participation and dialogue. It was a bold move—a deep reaffirmation that faith, while rooted in unwavering truths, must also be expressed in ways that are accessible and relatable to every generation.

This drive for renewal extended far beyond the walls of the Church. Paul VI embarked on extensive pastoral visits, traversing continents from Latin America to Africa and Asia. His travels, unprecedented for a modern pope, were not just symbolic gestures; they were opportunities for him to listen to diverse peoples' struggles, aspirations, and cultural expressions. In bustling urban centers and remote rural parishes, he met with community leaders, attended local services, and offered comfort to those whose lives had been upended by war, poverty, or political instability. In one memorable visit to a fractured industrial city in Italy—where local factories had given way to a new modern economy yet left many workers disenchanted—he spent several days conversing with organized labor, calling for social justice and protecting human dignity at every level. For many people, Paul VI's presence was uplifting—a reminder that the Church sought not only to dictate doctrine but to understand and address the everyday realities of life.

However, the path of reform was not smooth, and Paul VI's reign was deeply marked by both applause and bitter controversy. His encyclical Humanae Vitae (1968) was one of the most emphatic examples. With that document, Paul VI reaffirmed the Church's longstanding teachings on marriage, human sexuality, and contraception. In Humanae Vitae, the sanctity of life was exalted, and natural law was invoked as the basis for moral conduct. This position was meant to safeguard the integrity of the human person against the reduction of relationships to mere physical pleasure or utility. However, in an era that celebrated the freedoms unleashed by the sexual revolution and was increasingly informed by scientific inquiry into human biology, many critics viewed the encyclical as a stubborn, even repressive force. Heated debates ensued within parishes, seminaries, and academic forums. Television talk shows, university panels, and magazine editorials reflected the tension between a Church determined to hold fast to core principles and a culture eager to renegotiate long-held norms. For usual believers and fervent progressives alike, the encyclical became a focal point—a mirror reflecting the broader struggle between enduring tradition and the imperatives of contemporary life.

Throughout these public debates, Paul VI maintained an unwavering commitment to the pursuit of truth and the importance of ecclesiastical continuity. In his public addresses, he often spoke of the Church as a "great tree" with deep roots that must stretch its branches to embrace the winds of change. He argued passionately that reform was not an abandonment of faith but a maturation, a transformation that allowed the Church to be timeless and timely. His visionary approach was further exemplified in his calls for ecumenical and interfaith dialogue. Recognizing that the modern world was a tapestry woven from myriad religious and cultural threads, he reached out to leaders of other Christian denominations and Jewish, Muslim, Buddhist, and Hindu communities. Through global conferences and bilateral meetings, he championed that moral truth was not the exclusive property of any one tradition but a universal treasure that the insights of many could enrich. Such endeavors convinced many that the Church had evolved from an insular institution into a dynamic participant in the moral dialogue of the modern world.

In private correspondence, Paul VI's reflections voice the personal cost of carrying the hopes of millions during such transformative times. In later-circulated letters, he revealed the constant tension he experienced between the responsibilities of retaining cherished doctrines and the pressure to modernize and adapt. "In every step toward progress," he confided to a trusted aide, "I feel the weight of legacy and the silent cry of tradition calling me back. Nevertheless, we must dare to walk forward to illuminate the path for those who come after us." These intimate missives show a leader deeply conscious of the contradictions inherent in modern moral discourse: the desire to respect heritage while boldly confronting the new moral dilemmas of our age—from promises of technological utopia to threats of ethical decay.

As the winds of change raged outside the familiar stone walls of Rome, the Church itself was forced to grapple with internal schisms. Some clergy felt that the reforms diluted centuries of sacred tradition, while others embraced the spirit of dialogue and renewal that Paul VI so fervently promoted. In academies and parish halls, debates raged over the very nature of morality and the extent to which human freedom should be cherished versus restrained. These discussions, part of an ongoing internal dialogue within the Church, were critical in reconfiguring the identity of Catholicism. The outcome was a synthesis—a middle ground that acknowledged the necessity of continued doctrinal faithfulness while accepting that rigid adherence to old forms could leave the Church vulnerable to irrelevance in an age of rampant information and dynamic social change.

Technological advances during this era also enormously impacted how these issues were debated and disseminated among the faithful. The advent of television and radio transformed the papal office from a distant, abstract figurehead to a visible, relatable presence in everyday life. Paul VI's televised addresses, broadcast from the hallowed spaces of Rome's basilicas, allowed millions around the globe to witness a pope who was at once intellectual, empathetic, and extraordinarily human. His appearances reached audiences in far-flung lands and helped narrow the distance between the Church's leaders and congregants. The immediacy of his broadcasts and the subsequent public debate they spurred played a crucial role in how the Church responded to emerging challenges, ensuring that the dialogue between tradition and modernity was a lived, continuous experience rather than a static policy debate confined to the velvet-draped chambers of the Vatican.

Chapter Nineteen

1978 to current Banking Irregularities and the Mob.

In the late 1970s, the financial operations of the Vatican—long shrouded in secrecy and built upon centuries-old practices—found themselves at a crossroads. With the brief papacy of John Paul I in 1978, the Church's internal dynamics took an unexpected turn. His sudden and mysterious death shortly after his election ignited a maelstrom of speculation. Some conspiracy theories argue that John Paul I's unexpected demise was related to his reputed desire to reform the Vatican Bank (officially known as the Institute for Works of Religion, or IOR) and address longstanding financial irregularities. Although nothing was definitively proven, the echoes of these suspicions would soon be amplified by subsequent scandals that linked the Church's clandestine financial operations to organized crime and irregular banking practices.

Throughout the early 1980s, the shadow of these suspicions grew ever darker with the unraveling of the Banco Ambrosiano scandal.

This scandal would become emblematic of the toxic nexus between ecclesiastical finance, international banking, and the criminal underworld. Banco Ambrosiano, a bank with historical ties to the Vatican that had long been involved in cross-border financial activities, came under intense scrutiny when it was revealed that vast sums of money had been channeled to offshore accounts and dubious financial vehicles. The bank's operations, already marred by previous allegations of money laundering, were further implicated by its association with Propaganda Due (P2), an illicit Masonic lodge known to have ties with the Italian mafia and various political groups. At the center of this affair, the enigmatic figure of Roberto Calvi emerged. As the chairman of Banco Ambrosiano, Calvi's methods and his eventual mysterious death—his body found hanging in circumstances that many believed were engineered by organized crime—became emblematic of the potential for abuse inherent in a system that operated beyond the checks and balances of modern financial oversight.

During this period, the Vatican Bank was managed under the leadership of influential figures such as Cardinal Paul Marcinkus, whose tenure (roughly from 1971 to 1989) was marked by a persistent association with controversial bankers and criminal networks. Marcinkus, often seen as the figurehead of the IOR during its most tumultuous years, was reported to have worked closely with notorious banker Michele Sindona. Sindona's management of the bank involved practices that were later characterized by severe financial mismanagement, dubiously large sums of money flowing through the institution, and alleged facilitation of money laundering operations—activities that many observers believed provided an opening for organized crime to infiltrate the higher echelons of Vatican finance. The interplay between the ambitions of these financial operators, the bureaucratic culture of unquestioned secrecy, and the broader landscape of political and criminal intrigue in Italy created an environment in which illicit financial transactions could thrive under the nominal authority of the Church.

The Banco Ambrosiano affair was not an isolated incident; it formed part of a broader pattern of irregularities that would continue to plague the Vatican's financial institutions for decades. As investigators and journalists in Italy and abroad began to piece together the connections, a picture emerged of a financial network where large sums of money moved with little transparency, some of it allegedly funneled through covert channels to support ventures that straddled the line between legitimate commerce and outright criminality. Allegations abounded that funds from the Vatican Bank were being diverted to cover up the intricate financial arrangements of mafia groups, as well as to bribe or influence key political figures. These revelations, combined with the dramatic downfall of Banco Ambrosiano and the suspicious circumstances surrounding Calvi's death, fueled public outrage and a determined call for reform within a traditionally impervious institution.

As the years progressed into the 1990s and the dawn of the new millennium, the Vatican had neither forgotten nor entirely escaped its troubled past. Although the leadership of the Church sought to distance itself from the baggage of previous decades—initiating limited reforms and installing new oversight mechanisms—persistent allegations of mismanagement continued to surface. During these years, investigative reports and internal whistleblower accounts began to draw more explicit connections between the Vatican Bank's opaque financial practices and organized crime. Though definitive evidence was elusive—owing partly to the Vatican's longstanding tradition of financial confidentiality and partly to the sophisticated methods employed by those intent on deflecting scrutiny—documented cases of money laundering, bribery, and suspicious financial transfers left little doubt that irregular practices persisted well into the later twentieth century. These operations, it was alleged, had enabled criminal organizations to operate with a degree of impunity, exploiting loopholes in international banking regulations and taking advantage of the unique status of a sovereign state that is, in many respects, exempt from conventional financial oversight.

In response to the enduring scandals and the mounting internal pressures to overhaul its financial systems, the early twenty-first century proved to be an era of attempted transformation for the Vatican. Under the aegis of Pope Benedict XVI and, more vigorously, Pope Francis, a series of comprehensive reforms were initiated to target the heart of the institution's financial secrecy. Pope Francis, in particular, was outspoken about his determination to cleanse the Church's financial operations, launching initiatives that sought to bring greater transparency, accountability, and modern governance standards to the IOR. These reforms included stringent measures for independent audits, the restructuring of the bank's management, and efforts to align the institution's practices with international standards aimed at combating money laundering and financial terrorism. Nevertheless, even as modern auditing techniques and improved regulatory frameworks were introduced, critics maintained that the vestiges of the old guard—networks of contacts nurtured during earlier decades—continued to exert undue influence, calling into question whether actual change had been achieved or whether the problems were merely kept out of the public eye.

Despite these reform efforts, the legacy of past irregularities has proven to be remarkably tenacious. Contemporary investigations reveal that the Vatican Bank's challenges are as much about cultural inertia built over centuries as individual malfeasance. The very attributes that once allowed the institution to operate in relative secrecy—its status as a sovereign entity, the insulation provided by ecclesiastical tradition, and the reluctance to subject its internal affairs to external scrutiny—have become obstacles in the modern era, where transparency and accountability have reached a crescendo. In this context, even as the IOR has reportedly improved its internal controls, allegations persist that money continues to be diverted through complex networks involving offshore accounts, shell companies, and—according to some sources—even direct or indirect channels that have ties to organized crime. The intricate dance between tradition and modernity, secrecy and openness, continues to define the ongoing saga of Vatican finances in a world where criminal enterprises have become increasingly adept at exploiting the gaps in international regulation.

Within this tangled network of historical scandals and ongoing controversies, the intersections between organized crime and Vatican financial activities have not been confined solely to isolated episodes of mismanagement. Instead, they have also been intertwined with global geopolitical interests and clandestine alliances, with some accounts even implicating intelligence agencies, such as the CIA, in covert operations that intersected with the Church's accumulating financial resources. Documents and testimonies have suggested that, at various points, the Vatican's financial channels may have been used knowingly or inadvertently to facilitate transactions that supported political operations and covert interventions. These allegations, though difficult to substantiate in full due to the layers of secrecy governing both intelligence work and ecclesiastical finance, contribute to a broader narrative wherein the historical power of the Church as both a spiritual and an economic entity is shown to be susceptible to the temptations of unrestrained financial influence and the corrosive effects of criminal investment.

The repercussions of these financial irregularities have resonated far beyond the immediate sphere of Church operations. For many observers, the intricate connections between the Vatican Bank, organized crime, and international financial networks have become a case study of the perils of unchecked financial power in a modern globalized economy. The collateral damage of these irregularities has been felt in Italy, where political instability, corruption, and even occasional acts of violence have been linked to the murky underbelly of criminal finance. Moreover, the scandals have eroded public trust not only in a venerable institution but also in the broader systems of governance that were supposed to safeguard against the abuse of money and power. International regulatory bodies, including the Financial Action Task Force (FATF), have long singled out the Vatican's financial operations as needing reform, and the institution's unique status has posed particular challenges to efforts to ensure comprehensive transparency and accountability.

The struggle to reconcile centuries of tradition with the demands of modern financial oversight is further complicated by the inherent duality of the Vatican's mission. On the one hand, the Church is tasked with safeguarding the spiritual well-being of millions, a duty that, in many ways, benefits from a degree of confidentiality and autonomy. On the other hand, its role as a significant player in international finance—managing endowments, charitable donations, and the assets entrusted to it from around the globe—places it in a position where adherence to contemporary regulatory standards is essential. The tension between these two imperatives has often meant that even well-intentioned reform efforts can be undermined by bureaucratic inertia or entrenched networks reluctant to relinquish old behavior patterns. Such is the paradox that continues to haunt the Vatican: the very measures of discretion and separation that once defined its operational ethos now impede the much-needed transparency demanded by our modern era.

Technological advancements have added further complexity to the oversight of Vatican finances in recent years. While digitalization promises enhanced control and real-time monitoring of transactions, it also opens up new avenues for sophisticated money laundering and cyber-enabled financial crimes. The advent of cryptocurrencies, in particular, has presented both opportunities and risks for institutions like the IOR. On the one hand, blockchain technologies could theoretically promote greater transparency through immutable ledgers; on the other hand, they offer criminal elements an additional, often anonymous, channel through which funds can be moved without detection. In this evolving landscape, the Vatican has been forced to engage with international banking regulators and cybersecurity experts to ensure that its reforms are not rendered ineffective by the rapid pace of technological change—a challenge that underscores the enduring relevance of the issues first brought to light in the turbulent era of the late 1970s and 1980s.

Despite the sweeping reforms instituted by successive popes, including measures aimed at isolating and dismantling the exploitative networks of the past, the legacy of mob influence and financial mismanagement persists in the collective memory of both internal and external observers of the Church. Critics argue that while the outward appearances of transparency have improved, many deep-rooted practices that once allowed illicit financial activities to flourish have adapted to a new regulatory environment. The ongoing challenge, they insist, is not merely the elimination of individual scandals but the transformation of an entire culture that, for centuries, has seen significant sums of money operate in the shadows of dogma and secrecy. As long as vestiges of that shadow remain, the risk of recurrence looms, and the holy institution finds itself under continual internal reform and external pressure to justify its ancient, immensely influential financial architecture.

Looking to the future, the Vatican's struggle to completely eradicate the legacy of its past financial irregularities offers a sobering lesson in the interplay between institutional tradition and the imperatives of modern accountability. The continued efforts of reform-minded leaders within the Church, alongside persistent scrutiny from international regulators, signal a commitment to a more transparent and ethically sound financial practice. Nevertheless, the challenges are immense. The disruption of old networks—built on secrecy, loyalty, and, at times, the tacit cooperation of criminal enterprises—requires changes in procedures and a fundamental shift in the governance culture that has defined the Vatican for centuries. With every new technological innovation and every revised regulation, the Church is reminded that its historical entanglements with organized crime and irregular banking are not relics of a bygone era but ongoing realities that must be addressed with diligence, transparency, and an openness to change that transcends the weight of tradition.

In the final analysis, the period from 1978 to the present stands as a vivid illustration of how the intersections of money, power, and faith can give rise to a multifaceted crisis—one that encompasses not only financial mismanagement and deep-seated corruption but also a broader societal reckoning with the notions of accountability and transparency in a globalized world. The several high-profile scandals, from the mysterious circumstances surrounding a pope's brief tenure and tragic death to the enduring enigmas of Banco Ambrosiano, Roberto Calvi, and the murky dealings of the Vatican Bank, all contribute to a narrative that is as cautionary as it is compelling. The enduring saga of these events serves as a reminder that no institution, no matter how venerable its traditions, is immune to the corrupting influences of unregulated power and unaccountable money. Meanwhile, as historians, investigative journalists, regulators, and members of the faithful alike continue to probe and piece together the layers of this convoluted history, one truth persists unmistakably: the reconciliation of sacred purpose with transparent, ethical finance remains one of the most formidable challenges of our time.

Ultimately, what emerges from this longstanding struggle is a narrative that is as much about transformation as it is about transgression. In its efforts to extricate itself from a legacy riddled with allegations of mob influence and financial irregularity, the Vatican has embarked on a path fraught with both setbacks and promising signs of renewed accountability. Nevertheless, the journey remains incomplete. As new financial technologies evolve and international oversight becomes ever more rigorous, the Church's financial institutions will continue to be tested—not only by the residual specters of past scandals but also by the dynamic challenges of a modern global economy. In confronting these issues head-on, the Vatican may yet redefine the parameters of institutional reform and offer a blueprint for reconciling centuries of tradition with the imperatives of contemporary transparency and integrity. With its relentless demand for accountability, the modern era may thus prove to be the crucible in which the enduring tensions between the sacred and the profane are ultimately resolved.

This longstanding narrative, from the late 1970s to today, is emblematic of the broader, perennial conflict between secrecy and openness, between the allure of unchecked power and the rigorous demands of accountability. It is a story as layered and intricate as the institutions it describes—a story in which every financial irregularity, every whispered link to organized crime, and every bold attempt at reform contributes to a continuously evolving tapestry. While the shadows of past scandals still extend over the hallowed halls of the Vatican, the ongoing efforts to secure a more transparent future signal a commitment to change that resonates far beyond the confines of a single institution. For anyone interested in the interplay of religion, finance, and power, the saga of the Vatican Bank is a potent reminder that even in the realm of sacred institutions, the forces of human ambition and the lure of clandestine enrichment are never far away.

In sum, from 1978 onward, this period remains a critical chapter in the complex history of Vatican finances, a chapter marked by scandal, reform, and the unyielding quest for transparency in an area that has long been characterized by mystery and intrigue. The interplay of mob influence, the machinations of unscrupulous bankers, and the enduring impact of institutional practices rooted in centuries of secrecy offers a cautionary tale and an insightful case study on the challenges of modernizing ancient institutions. As ongoing investigations and continual reforms strive to lift the veil on these enduring controversies, the historical record grows richer, providing scholars and the public with valuable lessons on the corrosive effects of unbridled power and the redemptive potential of steadfast accountability.

Conclusion

Reflections on Continuity, Change, and Papal Leadership

As we close this journey through the corridors of papal history, we are left with a sweeping panorama—a grand tapestry woven from the fervent threads of divine aspiration, crushing human frailty, courageous testimony, and moments of moral compromise. Our exploration has carried us from the grim, often macabre, manifestations of power in medieval times, when sacred authority was wielded to assert temporal dominion in brutal, unyielding ways, to the magnificent yet tumultuous struggles that later reshaped humankind's very understanding of the cosmos in the wake of conflicts between faith and emerging scientific insight. In every era—from the shadowed courts of early popes and the horrifying spectacle of the Cadaver Synod to the modern, reforming spirit embodied by figures like Pope Paul VI—we have witnessed how the great mantle of papal authority, though conceived as a divine mandate, has always been indelibly marked by the limitations and imperfections of its human bearers.

The Enduring Stain of Human Nature

In the medieval age, the papacy was inexorably linked to a world of feudal politics and ruthless ambition. The institution that once claimed an unassailable moral high ground was forced repeatedly into the arena of power struggles, where the pursuit of prestige and territorial conquest often trumped the exalted ideals of spiritual leadership. The grotesque affair of the Cadaver Synod—an event in which a deceased pope was exhumed and put on trial—stands as a stark emblem of this era. Though the spectacle shocked later generations, it epitomized a time when the sacred and the profane were indistinguishably intertwined. Even as it aroused horror, the event set a lasting precedent: no institution, however divinely mandated, could entirely escape the pervasive stains of corruption or the demands of political and familial ambitions. In that crucible of ambition, brutality, and power, the Church learned early on that its lofty ideals were forever bound to the messy realities of human nature. This lesson would reverberate down the centuries.

Faith, Reason, and Reformation

Our journey then sweeps forward into the age of intellectual awakening, when the challenge posed by emerging scientific thought began to unsettle long-held ecclesiastical doctrines. The iconic stand of Galileo Galilei, who dared to question the Aristotelian celestial order that underpinned Church teachings, epitomizes the eternal conflict between revelation and reason. It was not merely a clash over astronomical models; Galileo's bold defiance in pursuing empirical truth called into question the very foundation upon which the Church had built its claims to divine insight. The ensuing controversy—marked by condemnations, prohibitions, and rigorous maintenance of orthodoxy—was both a lament for lost certainty and an impetus for transformation. This turbulent period reminds us that the evolution of human understanding often emerges from the tension between old doctrines and new discoveries, a process that, though painful, ultimately enriches our collective capacity for progress.

As the pages of history turned toward the era of the Counter-Reformation, the papacy was forced to reckon with its internal weaknesses in the wake of the seismic Protestant Reformation. In response to the turmoil brought on by the challenges of Martin Luther and other reformers, the Church, under leaders like Paul IV and Urban VIII, resorted to measures that bordered on the draconian. Inquisitions, excommunications, and harsh decrees were deployed to purge heresy and reestablish a semblance of order. Here, too, we discern a recurring theme in the Church's long and tortuous saga: the immense difficulty of balancing preserving sacred tradition and adapting to the demands for change. Although these severe measures deepened internal strife and sowed the seeds of further conflict, they also catalyzed an introspective process that eventually paved the way for a more mature and self-critical institution.

Confronting Totalitarianism and Embracing Modernity

The crucible of conflict continued into the turbulent interwar years, when Pope Pius XI confronted the formidable rise of totalitarian regimes. Faced with the brutal realities of Nazi Germany and Fascist Italy, the Church was forced into a perilous negotiation between collaboration and resistance. Treaties like the Reichskonkordat and the Lateran Treaty, though intended as shields of temporary protection, ultimately proved inadequate to stave off the moral and political corruption that threatened to engulf the institution. Out of this oppressive milieu emerged the encyclical Mit Brennender Sorge, an incisive and understated condemnation of the Nazi ideology—a quiet yet resolute call to awaken the moral consciousness of a nation submerged in tyranny. In these moments of desperate compromise, the Church demonstrated that despite overwhelming political might, a steadfast commitment to timeless values could kindle the embers of defiance.

Emerging from the devastation of global conflict, the papacy embraced yet another period of profound transformation under the dynamic leadership of Pope Paul VI. In the aftermath of World War II and amid the sweeping reforms of the Second Vatican Council,

Paul VI set about reimagining the Church's role in a rapidly mod-ernizing world. From 1963 to 1978, his tenure was characterized by a deliberate duality: hopeful openness to new ideas and dialogues, even as he maintained a vigilant defense of the Church's foundational doctrines. Through liturgical reforms, groundbreaking ecumenical outreach, and his historic journeys to distant lands, Paul VI sought to bridge the gap between the sacred past and the intertwined challenges of contemporary society. Nevertheless, his legacy, too, was marred by controversy. The fierce global debates ignited by the encyclical Humanae Vitae, which reaffirmed traditional teachings on marriage and sexuality, laid bare the internal struggles that persisted even as the Church sought outward renewal. His era remains emblematic of a continual negotiation—a dynamic synthesis of vision, tradition, and an enduring commitment to uphold moral principles in the face of relentless change.

The Persistent Shadows: Vatican Finances

Taken together, the sweeping chapters of papal history reveal an in-stitution that, despite its divine aspirations, was never immune to the flaws of its human stewards. From the medieval courts rife with vio-lence and ambition to the fires of scientific and theological inquiry, and from the harsh rigidity of the Counter-Reformation to the cau-tious reawakening of modernity, the papacy has always reflected the complexities and contradictions inherent in human leadership. Each pope—whether condemned for acts of brutal retribution, venerated for their courage in challenging orthodoxy, or revered for visionary reforming an outdated structure—serves as a poignant reminder that the highest callings are not measured by pristine perfection but by the willingness to embrace the struggle, to learn from error, and to strive for redemption even amid profound imperfection.

In contemplating this grand historical panorama, we are reminded that the history of the papacy is not a linear progression of immutable virtues but rather an odyssey marked by moments of moral despair alongside bursts of courageous defiance. This epic narrative, with its valleys of dark corruption and peaks of transcendent redemption, teaches us that institutions of power—no matter how divinely in- spired—must continually adapt or risk falling prey to the accumu- lative scars of human frailty. Moreover, it challenges our contempo- rary notions of leadership and morality. In an age marked by rapid change and complex ethical dilemmas, the struggles and triumphs of popes past provide enduring lessons on the necessity of maintaining a delicate equilibrium between upholding eternal truths and engaging earnestly with the shifting realities of the modern world.

The Monsters Within: A Deeper Reflection on Human Nature

The story that unfolds before us testifies to the inescapable truth that no institution, however venerable or divinely ordained, can remain unblemished by the inevitable imperfection of its human components. The popes we encountered over the centuries were not statues of flawlessness; they were deeply human figures, burdened by the weight of history and the constraints of their time and humanity. Their grand ambitions, often set against impersonal forces of political expediency, highlight the constant negotiation between lofty ideals and the complex realities of mortal existence. However, beneath these imperfections burns a resilient spark—a hopeful conviction that the quest for a higher truth remains ever possible through the vigorous process of struggle, reflection, and transformation.

Indeed, as we reflect on the pervasive human flaws evident throughout papal history—the unchecked ambition, the fear, the struggle for control—we come to understand these not merely as individual failings but as manifestations of deeper, often unconscious human impulses. Just as Lincoln spoke of the "better angels of our nature," history also reveals the "worst side of our devils," the powerful, instinctive drives that reside beneath our "everyday persona." In psychological terms, these can be understood as "monsters emerging from the Id"—visceral symbols of the unconscious desires, fears, and impulses that are largely hidden from our conscious mind. When these impulses are repressed or unintegrated, they frequently manifest as "monsters" in our dreams, art, literature, or cultural myths. These monstrous figures are not simply aberrations of fantasy; they function as powerful archetypes that reflect the inner turmoil of our suppressed emotions, providing vivid metaphors for aspects of our identity that we may find too overwhelming or dangerous to face directly.

Within our narratives, these monstrous projections serve to highlight the shadow side of our humanity, the part of us that is capable of irrational fear, uncontrolled aggression, and forbidden desire. When these repressed forces bubble to the surface, they profoundly shape our experience, whether by fueling nightmares that force us to face our deepest anxieties or inspiring creative expression that gives voice to our hidden emotional landscapes. The imagery of monsters—unearthly beings with distorted, often terrifying forms such as the devil—arise as a projection of our internal conflicts; they stand as both warnings and invitations, challenging us to recognize that our humanity is not composed solely of reason and order, but also of chaos and untamed passion.

On a collective level, these "monsters of the Id" take on cultural significance as well. They permeate folklore, mythology, and modern media, symbolizing the uncontrollable forces of nature and the darker elements of the human psyche. Throughout history, societies have employed monstrous imagery to articulate a sense of unease about the unknown and the transgressive aspects of human behavior. Whether in the form of dragons, demons, or other creatures of the night, these figures remind communities of the omnipresent threat of chaos lurking beyond the bounds of civilization. They serve as cautionary tales, reinforcing social norms by externalizing what must remain in the depths of our suppressed selves. In doing so, they also encourage a reflection on what it means to be human—in all its multifaceted, conflicted, and sometimes contradictory glory.

On an individual level, encountering these monsters—whether in dreams, therapeutic settings, or artistic endeavors—encourages a journey of self-discovery and integration. Acknowledging and reconciling with one's inner darkness is a crucial developmental task. Drawing on Jungian ideas, integrating the shadow, which can be seen as the embodiment of these monstrous elements, is vital for achieving psychological wholeness. By confronting our monsters, we can transform fear into insight and irrationality into creative power. This alchemical process of metamorphosing raw, chaotic energy into a source of personal strength is essential, as it reclaims parts of ourselves that have long been exiled to the unconscious, enriching our capacity for empathy, resilience, and authentic self-expression.

Beyond individual psychology, these monstrous manifestations pervasively influence the collective human experience, molding social attitudes and cultural narratives. They are both a mirror and a mediator, reflecting the suppressed collective anxieties of entire communities and often serving as catalysts for social change. Political movements, moral panics, and mass cultural phenomena sometimes draw upon the language of monsters to articulate fears about corruption, loss of identity, or societal breakdown. The power of this imagery lies in its ability to encapsulate complex emotional and psychological states in a visceral, almost tangible form. In doing so, these monstrous symbols facilitate a dialogue about control limits, the necessity of acknowledging our innate vulnerabilities, and the ongoing tension between individual freedom and collective responsibility.

At the same time, creative fields such as literature, cinema, visual arts, and music have long harnessed the potency of monstrous imagery to question conventional wisdom and explore the labyrinthine depths of the human condition. Artists and storytellers draw on these archetypal figures to probe the paradoxes of beauty and terror, order and chaos, progress and regression—the underlying duality in everything we do. In this way, monsters from the Id are not merely objects of dread but also instigators of catharsis and innovation. They encourage us to question societal taboos and explore alternative modes of being, ultimately contributing to an evolving cultural consciousness that values the integration of all aspects of the self.

Thus, the monsters from the Id shape human experience, serving as constant reminders of the dual nature of our existence—a delicate balance between the light of rationality and the dark reservoirs of instinct. Their persistent presence in our inner lives and cultural expressions challenges us to embrace complexity, reconcile the conflicting forces within, and recognize that the path to genuine self-understanding often winds through the landscapes of fear and desire we would otherwise avoid. In confronting these monsters, we reveal the depths of our psyche and expand the narrative of what it means to be human, acknowledging that every act of creativity, every moment of insight, carries with it the echoes of our most profound and enigmatic impulses.

A Continuing Legacy

Let us then take to heart the lessons of this grand odyssey: that through struggle, introspection, and unwavering determination, even the most revered institutions can transform their darkest chapters into beacons of hope for future generations. In that spirit, the legacy of the popes—each a testament to both the sublime and the flawed—urges us to persist in our quest for truth, justice, and a more compassionate future.

As we close this epic journey through the annals of papal history, we are left with a resonant and, indeed, liberating truth: that while our imperfect, mortal nature forever mars the pursuit of divine truth, it is precisely in our striving—and in our willingness to confront unpleasant truths—that we find the possibility for genuine transformation. From the medieval era to the modern age, the popes have shown us that the path to a more enlightened future is paved with both luminous moments of courage and the humbling recognition of our fallibility. In this courageous interplay between the eternal and the ephemeral, between sacred command and human flaw, lies the lasting legacy of the papacy—a legacy that continues to illuminate our ongoing quest for meaning, justice, and redemption in a complex, ever-changing world.

May the pages of Shadows & Sanctity serve as both scholarly inquiry and a mirror to our struggles—an ongoing conversation between the ideals we hold dear and the realities we must confront.

Afterword

The Unfolding Human Story

In Shadows & Sanctity, we've traversed centuries of controversy, witnessing the interplay of divine obligation and human ambition. The legacy of these popes, with all their splendor and scandal, offers a window into the eternal struggle between the lofty ideals of spiritual leadership and the unyielding reality of human imperfection. As the dialogue between sanctity and scandal continues to evolve in our own time, may this work serve as both an inquiry into our past and a guide for thoughtful reflection about our future.

Thank you for embarking on this journey through history's most challenging and compelling chapters. Within these narratives, the story of the papacy stands as a vibrant, evolving testament to the intricate interplay of faith, power, and humanity. This living account not only chronicles the profound influence of religious leadership over the centuries but also offers a powerful counterpoint to the existential rumination found in Shakespeare's Macbeth. In Act 5, Scene 5, Macbeth laments:

"Tomorrow, and tomorrow, and tomorrow, Creeps in this petty pace from day to day, To the last syllable of recorded time; And all our yesterdays have lighted fools The way to dusty death. Out, out, brief candle! Life's but a walking shadow, a poor player That struts and frets his hour upon the stage And then is heard no more: it is a tale Told by an idiot, full of sound and fury, signifying nothing."

This evocative passage encapsulates the endless dualism at the very heart of the human condition—a duality endlessly debated yet often stymied by the inherent limitations of our human experience. Here, the stark declaration that life is "a tale told by an idiot, full of sound and fury, signifying nothing" unveils Macbeth's profound sense of nihilism. The "idiot" he describes represents not merely foolishness but also the inherent absurdity and sometimes the senselessness of human endeavors. Despite the ceaseless clamor and vigorous pursuits that define our lives, what often endures is little more than an overwhelming burst of chaos and emotional display that ultimately signifies emptiness.

In this light, the phrase "sound and fury" conjures an image of vigorous, impassioned activity and dramatic intensity that, when all is said and done, amounts to only transient noise. Shakespeare seems to warn that even the grand gestures, the intense passions, and the dramatic highs and lows of our lives might ultimately dissolve into the ephemeral void—a reminder that our deepest aspirations and fears, no matter how loud, may fade into insignificance against the relentless passage of time.

Yet, when we juxtapose this nihilistic reflection against the narrative of the papacy, a different story emerges—one of enduring legacy, complex power, and the transformative role of faith. The papacy's history is not simply a chronicle of religious dogma or ritual; it is an ongoing dialogue about the reconciliation of human ambition with the quest for spiritual truth. Even as debates rage over the meaning, or seeming meaninglessness, of our endeavors, the unfolding chapters of history—steeped in tradition, conflict, and renewal—offer a testament to the enduring complexity that shapes our human experience.

Thus, while Macbeth's soliloquy powerfully underscores the transient nature of life's passions as fleeting bursts of "sound and fury," the narrative of the papacy reminds us that within the ruins of past glories and follies there remain timeless questions of faith, power, and identity. These enduring questions, echoing through the corridors of time, invite us to look beyond the clamor of momentary emotions and to seek a deeper understanding of what truly endures in the human spirit. We will likely find endless debate with no clear answer or verifiable proof ever being found, leaving us with the ultimate conundrum of not knowing for certain. That ultimately is the human experience.

So, as we close this journey, we're left not with a neat resolution, but with a mirror. The papacy's imperfect history reflects our own inherent contradictions—the capacity for both profound good and grave error. It demands that we confront our own "sound and fury" and choose, with humility and courage, what we truly wish to signify.

About the Author

Allen Schery is a philosophical anthropologist, historian, author, and museum designer with a profound and diverse background spanning archaeology, anthropology, and historical research. He has excavated Maya ruins at Chichen Itza and lived among preliterate groups to deepen his understanding of the human experience across cultures and epochs. Drawing on over fifty years of research, Schery has authored several interdisciplinary works including "Sanctity and Shadows – The Unholy See," a detailed historical examination of controversial papal history, and "The Shattered Cross – The Rise, Fall and Undying Legacy of the Knights Templars." He also authored philosophical-anthropological texts on human nature such as "The Dragons Breath – The Human Experience" and "The Primate Principle."

Beyond writing, Allen is an avid collector and curator of memorabilia, notably focusing on the Brooklyn Dodgers. He designed a 46,000 square foot museum to house his Dodger collection and has been instrumental in researching the origins of the Dodgers, uncovering new historical insights into their founding. His museum design credits include the Corvette Americana Museum in Cooperstown, New York, the Dodger Experience Museum at Dodger Stadium, and the Rose Bowl Museum in Pasadena.

His multidisciplinary expertise merges rigorous scholarship with creative storytelling, as seen in his recently completed book and movie script, "The Mystery of the Ark," which blends historical speculation with thriller elements inspired by Dan Brown and Hitchcockian twists. Schery's work stands at the nexus of history, anthropology, and cultural inquiry, offering both academic insights and engaging narratives that illuminate complex human experiences and institutional histories.

Allen Schery combines a deeply analytical mind with a passion for storytelling and cultural preservation, making his contributions to literature and museum design uniquely rich and impactful.

Bibliography

Sources and Helpful Notes

Preface

• Early Catholic Church Popes:

o Historical records from Eusebius of Caesarea's Church History

o Writings of early Church Fathers such as Irenaeus and Tertullian

• Apocrypha:

o Various lists of biblical books written before the Council of Nicaea

o Early Christian texts like the Gospel of Thomas and Shepherd of Hermas

• Constantine:

o Life of Constantine by Eusebius

o Letters from Constantine before and after the Council of Nicaea

• Council of Nicaea (325 AD):

o Decoding Nicea by Paul Pavao

o Historical sources from Eusebius, Socrates Scholasticus, and Theodoret

191

• Council of Milan:

o Records from the reign of Emperor Constantine and his policies on Christianity

o Church documents discussing the enforcement of Nicene Christianity

Here are some of the sources related to the Council of Milan (AD 355):

• Historical Records: The council was summoned by Emperor Constantius II and dealt with the condemnation of Athanasius. Key figures included Eusebius of Vercelli and Lucifer of Cagliari.

Ancient Descriptions: Writings from Hilary, Athanasius, Rufinus, Socrates Scholasticus, and Theodoret provide insights into the council's events and decisions.

• Surviving Documents: A letter to Eusebius of Vercelli is one of the few remaining documents from the council.

Chapter One

• Encyclopædia Britannica – "Pope Joan" Offers a critical analysis of the legends surrounding Pope Joan, evaluating the historical evidence (or lack thereof) and the evolution of her myth over time.

• Jean de Mailly's Chronicle (circa 1250) One of the earliest sources mentioning the female pope, providing the foundation on which later embellishments were built.

• Martin of Opava's "Chronicon Pontificum et Imperatorum" A 13th century chronicle that adds significant details to the Pope Joan narrative, contributing to its widespread dissemination in medieval Europe.

Chapter Two

• JSTOR The Cadaver Synod: Putting a Dead Pope on Trial - JSTOR Daily

• Joseph Cummings – History's Great Untold Stories: Covers unusual historical events, including the Cadaver Synod.

• Horace Mann – The Catholic Encyclopedia: Provides a detailed account of Pope Stephen VI and the political intrigue surrounding the trial.

• Bartolomeo Platina – The Lives of the Popes: A historical work detailing the reigns of various popes, including Stephen VI.

• PopeHistory.com – Offers a historical overview of Pope Stephen VI and the Cadaver Synod.

Chapter Three

• The Great Schism: 1378 - John Holland Smith

• A Distant Mirror: The Calamitous 14th Century Barbara W. Tuchman

• The Great Schism-Francis Oakley

- The Western Schism and the Council of Constance: A Critical Examination-H.B. Workman

Chapter Four

- Encyclopædia Britannica – "Sergius III" Offers a concise, fact-checked summary of his papacy, detailing his background, his tumultuous rise to power, and his impact on Church politics during a turbulent era.

- The Oxford Dictionary of Popes (by J.N.D. Kelly) A scholarly resource that situates Pope Sergius III within the broader narrative of papal history, providing detailed biographical insights and analysis of the political and ecclesiastical dynamics of his time.

- Catholic Encyclopedia – "Pope Sergius III" Discusses his life and papacy from a traditional perspective, addressing both his political maneuvers and the personal scandals that have contributed to his controversial historical legacy.

Chapter Five

- Liutprand of Cremona's Antapodosis (958–962) – Provides firsthand accounts of papal politics during the 10th century.

- The Liber Pontificalis – A collection of biographies of popes, including details on John XII and Benedict IX.

- Records from the Saeculum Obscurum period – Discusses the political influence of Roman aristocratic families on the papacy.

• • Will Durant – Caesar and Christ, part of The Story of Civilization, which covers the Roman Empire and early Christianity.

• • Caesar Baronius – Annales Ecclesiastici, a monumental history of the Church from Christ to the 16th century.

• • The Synod of Sutri (1046) – This council deposed Pope Benedict IX, Pope Sylvester III, and Pope Gregory VI due to accusations of corruption and simony.

• • The Council of Constance (1414–1418) – Deposed Pope John XXIII and resolved the Western Schism by accepting Pope Gregory XII's resignation.

• • The Council of Pisa (1409) – Attempted to depose both Pope Gregory XII and Antipope Benedict XIII, though it was not universally recognized.

• • Canon Law on Papal Resignation – Codex Iuris Canonici (1983) outlines the process for a pope's voluntary resignation but does not explicitly address forced deposition.

• OnePeterFive - On Deposing Popes: A Historical Review: Examines historical cases of papal deposition and the theological debates surrounding them.

• Hungarian Conservative - Can a Pope be Legitimately Removed from the Papal Throne?: Discusses past instances of papal removal, including Pope Benedict IX and the Synod of Sutri.

Chapter Six

• Theocratic Centralism: The Politics of Boniface VIII – A seminar paper analyzing Pope Boniface VIII's political struggles and ambitions.

• Medieval Sourcebook - Fordham University – A collection of primary medieval texts, including documents related to papal politics.

• Urban Europe - The New Cambridge Medieval History – Discusses urban political power and the role of the papacy in medieval European cities

Chapter Seven

• Cesare Borgia - Renaissance and Reformation – A scholarly entry discussing Cesare Borgia's rise and political maneuvers.

• The Borgias: Scandalous Papal Family of Renaissance Rome – Covers the notorious history of the Borgia family, including Pope Alexander VI.

• Cancel Crusade: How Gossip and Scandal Ruined a Rare Renaissance Treasure – Examines the impact of Pope Alexander VI's reputation on Renaissance art.

• Johann Burchard's Chronicles/Accounts: These near-contemporary records offer firsthand descriptions of life in the Vatican, including vivid details of events like the Banquet of Chestnuts—even if later historians debate their accuracy.

• Niccolò Machiavelli's The Prince: This seminal work offers insight into the political tactics of Cesare Borgia. Machiavelli's analysis of power and realpolitik is invaluable for understanding the ruthless ambition behind the Borgia legacy.

• "The Borgias: The Hidden History" by G.J. Meyer: Meyer's work provides a comprehensive and well-researched narrative on the Borgia family, blending detailed historical accounts with an engaging storytelling style.

• "The Borgias: Power and Fortune" by Paul Strathern: Strathern's book offers a critical analysis of how the Borgias influenced Renaissance politics, exploring both their notorious excesses and their lasting impact on European history.

• "The Borgias: History's Most Notorious Dynasty" by Sarah Dunlap: Assuming this title (or similar titles by reputable historians on the Borgias) is available, it can serve as a resource for detailed reconstructions of events, personal scandals, and the broader historical context.

• Focused Biographies such as Pope Alexander VI: The Life and Legacy of Rodrigo Borgia by John Ferguson: This type of work digs deeply into the papal reign and offers a nuanced picture of Alexander VI's life—helpful for supporting detailed passages on his political maneuverings and personal controversies.

• "A History of the Papacy" by Eamon Duffy: Duffy's rigorous scholarly approach provides context for the Church's state during the Renaissance, shedding light on how controversies like those of the Borgias contributed to wider calls for reform.

Chapter Eight

• Saints & Sinners: A History of the Popes-Eamon Duffy

• The Popes: A History-John Julius Norwich

• The Oxford Dictionary of Popes-J.N.D. Kelly

• The Spanish Conquest of America and Its Relation to the Discovery of the New World-Lewis Hanke

• Bartolomé de las Casas: An Essay in Translation-Gustavo Gutiérrez

• A Short Account of the Destruction of the Indies-Bartolomé de las Casas (primary source, but available in many editions)

• The Laws of Burgos of 1512-1513: Royal Ordinances for the Good Government and Treatment of the Indians-Translated by Lesley Byrd Simpson (historical document collections)

• The Origins of International Law: Francisco de Vitoria and the School of Salamanca-James Brown Scott

• The Doctrine of Discovery: An Indigenous Perspective-Steven Newcomb

Chapter Nine

• "Key Figures of the Reformation: Pope Clement VII" –by Fr. Dwight Longenecker.

• "Clement VII | Biography, Papacy, & Facts" – Written and fact-checked by The Editors of Encyclopedia Britannica.

• "Roman Catholic Popes of the 16th Century" –by Austin Cline, a former regional director for the Council for Secular Humanism

Chapter Ten

• Records from the Roman Inquisition:

• Pope Paul IV expanded the Inquisition beyond Italy, particularly in Spain, where it became a tool for enforcing orthodoxy under King Philip II.

• The Index Librorum Prohibitorum (1559) was created under Paul IV to censor books deemed dangerous to faith and morals.

• Paul IV's papacy was marked by aggressive anti-Protestant policies, including his refusal to recognize the abdication of Emperor Charles V and the election of Ferdinand I.

• His papal bulls and decrees reinforced Catholic orthodoxy and intensified censorship.

• Pius IV reversed many of Paul IV's harsh policies, including reducing the severity of the Inquisition and relaxing censorship laws.

• The trial of the Carafa family—Paul IV's nephews—was a significant event in Pius IV's efforts to restore papal authority and distance himself from his predecessor's extreme measures.

Chapter Eleven

• Saints & Sinners: A History of the Popes-John Julius Norwich

• The Oxford Dictionary of Popes-J.N.D. Kelly

• A History of the Council of Trent-Hubert Jedin

• The Catholic Reformation-Pierre Janelle

• The Counter-Reformation: Catholic Europe and the Non-Christian World-H. Outram Evennett

• Trent and All That: Renaming Catholicism in the Early Modern Era-John W. O'Malley

• The Jesuits: A History from Ignatius to the Present-John W. O'Malley

• The Roman Catechism: Catechism of the Council of Trent-(Various published editions; often attributed to the Council of Trent itself, or to St. Charles Borromeo's influence in its compilation)

• The Canons and Decrees of the Council of Trent-(Various published translations, e.g., by H.J. Schroeder)

• St. John of the Cross (Translated by Kieran Kavanaugh, Otilio Rodriguez, or others)

• St. Teresa of Ávila (Translated by Kieran Kavanaugh, Otilio Rodriguez, or others)

• The Baroque: Architecture, Sculpture, Painting-Germain Bazin

• The Counter-Reformation, 1559-1610-Marvin R. O'Connell

Chapter Twelve

The Vatican summary of the trial against Bruno contains interrogations, abstracts of Bruno's works, and sentencing details.

• The Trials of Giordano Bruno (1592–1600) document his imprisonment, accusations, and final plea before the Holy Office.

Papal Decrees and Correspondence:

• Pope Clement VIII presided over Bruno's trial and issued strict measures against heresy, documented in Vatican records.

• Papal Artifacts from Clement VIII's era include official statements regarding religious orthodoxy.

Eyewitness Accounts:

• The Flames of Thought: Giordano Bruno's Final Stand describes the execution scene in Campo de' Fiori.

• The Trial of Giordano Bruno (2015) provides details on Bruno's final moments and his defiant response to the inquisitors.

• History Today recounts the events leading up to his execution and the Church's justification. Giordano Bruno Executed | History Today

Church Records:

• The Vatican Secret Archives hold a summary of Bruno's trial, which was kept secret for years before being published.

Chapter Thirteen

• Trial Documents of Galileo Galilei (1633) – Official records from the Roman Inquisition detailing Galileo's charges, defense, and sentencing.

• Papal Correspondence – Letters between Pope Urban VIII and Galileo, including discussions on heliocentrism and Church doctrine.

The Dialogue Concerning the Two Chief World Systems (1632) – Galileo's work that led to his trial, presenting arguments for and against the Copernican system.

• The Letter to the Grand Duchess Christina (1615) – Galileo's defense of heliocentrism and its compatibility with scripture.

• Records from the Vatican Archives – Documents detailing the Church's stance on Copernicanism and the enforcement of doctrinal orthodoxy.

Chapter Fourteen

• Qui Pluribus (1846) – An encyclical by Pius IX addressing faith, reason, and the dangers of modern ideologies. You can read it here.

• Syllabus of Errors (1864) – A document condemning various modern philosophical and political ideas, reinforcing traditional Catholic doctrine. More details here.

• Pastor Aeternus (1870) – A declaration from the First Vatican Council defining papal infallibility.

Chapter Fifteen

• Ad Beatissimi Apostolorum (1914) – Benedict XV's first encyclical, condemning the war and calling for peace.

• The Papal Peace Note (1917) – A formal proposal by Benedict XV urging an end to the war, describing it as "useless carnage."

• Records from the Vatican Archives – Documents detailing Benedict XV's diplomatic efforts and humanitarian initiatives.

• World War I Correspondence – Letters between Benedict XV and European leaders discussing peace negotiations.

• The Washington Naval Conference (1921–1922) – Benedict XV's support for post-war disarmament efforts

Chapter Sixteen

• Mit Brennender Sorge (1937) – An encyclical issued by Pius XI condemning Nazi ideology and violations of the Reichskonkordat. You can read it here.

• Reichskonkordat (1933) – A treaty between Nazi Germany and the Vatican, signed to protect Catholic institutions but later violated by the Nazi regime. More details here.

• Pius XI and Nazi Germany, 1937-1939 – A scholarly analysis of Pius XI's diplomatic struggles with Nazi Germany.

Chapter Seventeen

• Vatican Secret Archives – Pope Francis announced access to wartime documents in 2020, allowing researchers to examine Pius XII's actions during World War II.

• Mit Brennender Sorge (1937) – An encyclical issued by Pius XI, Pius XII's predecessor, condemning Nazi ideology, which Pius XII affirmed during his papacy.

• Reichskonkordat (1933) – A treaty between Nazi Germany and the Vatican, signed to protect Catholic institutions but later violated by the Nazi regime.

• The Pope at War: Pius XII and the Vatican's Secret Archives – A historical analysis of Pius XII's role during World War II, based on newly released Vatican documents.

• The Pius War: Responses to the Critics of Pius XII – This work, co-authored by William Doino and edited by Rabbi David G. Dalin, compiles extensive interviews, archival documents, and firsthand testimonies, specifically examining Pope Pius XII's efforts to rescue Jews and others persecuted by the Nazis.

Chapter Eighteen

• Humanae Vitae (1968) – An encyclical addressing birth control and Catholic teachings on human life.

• Evangelii Nuntiandi (1975) – A papal exhortation on evangelization in the modern world.

• Sacerdotalis Caelibatus (1967) – A document reaffirming the Church's stance on priestly celibacy.

• Documents from the Second Vatican Council (1962–1965) – Records detailing reforms that shaped Paul VI's papacy.

• Papal correspondence and decrees – Letters and official statements discussing morality, social justice, and Church doctrine.

Chapter Nineteen

• Italian Judicial Proceedings on the Banco Ambrosiano Scandal (Early 1980s):

• Court documents and trial transcripts from the investigations and legal proceedings surrounding Banco Ambrosiano. These records include evidence logs and witness testimonies that detail the involvement of key figures (such as Roberto Calvi) and expose links between irregular banking practices, organized crime, and the Vatican Bank.

• Vatican Bank (Institute for Works of Religion) Internal Reports and Financial Statements (1978–Present):

• Annual accounts, internal audit reports, and correspondence produced by the IOR. These documents provide firsthand financial records and insights into the bank's operational procedures during periods marked by scandals and allegations of mismanagement.

• Italian Parliamentary Commission Reports on Vatican Finances

• Investigative reports and testimonies compiled by Italian government bodies and Parliament.

• Calvi Trial Records:

• Legal documents include trial transcripts, depositions, and judicial findings from the court cases against Roberto Calvi. These records serve as primary evidence of how the financial misdeeds of Banco Ambrosiano intersected with organized crime and implicate links to the Vatican's financial institutions.

• Official Communications and Public Statements from the Holy See:

Press releases, apostolic letters, and official statements issued during or after major banking controversies. These documents, found in Vatican archives and official publications, provide the Church's perspective on the issues and outline subsequent reforms or defensive measures taken in response to the scandals.

Summary

Summary comes from synthesizing all the above sources. The summary regarding the Human Condition comes from my 2022 Book "The Dragon's Breath-The Human Experience" which took 50 years of analysis to complete.

Index

.Created with TExtract / www.TExtract.com]